NATIONAL GEOGRAPHIC DIRECTIONS

Sicilian Odyssey

FRANCINE PROSE

Sicilian Odyssey

NATIONAL GEOGRAPHIC DIRECTIONS

NATIONAL GEOGRAPHIC
Washington, D.C.

Published by the National Geographic Society
1145 17th Street, N.W., Washington, D.C. 20036-4688

Library of Congress Cataloging-in-Publication Data

Prose, Francine, 1947 -
    Sicilian odyssey / Francine Prose.
      p. cm. -- (National Geographic directions)
    ISBN 0-7922-6535-1 (hc.)
    1. Sicily (Italy)–Description and travel. 2. Prose, Francine,
1947--Journeys--Italy--Sicily. I. Title. II. Series.

    DG864.3.P76 2003
    914.5'80493–dc21

                                                    2002044379

One of the world's largest nonprofit scientific and educational organizations, the National Geographic
Society was founded in 1888 "for the increase and diffusion of geographic knowledge." Fulfilling this
mission, the Society educates and inspires millions every day through its magazines, books, television
programs, videos, maps and atlases, research grants, the National Geographic Bee, teacher workshops,
and innovative classroom materials. The Society is supported through membership dues, charitable
gifts, and income from the sale of its educational products. This support is vital to National
Geographic's mission to increase global understanding and promote conservation of our planet
through exploration, research, and education.

For more information, please call 1-800-NGS LINE (647-5463), write to the Society at the above
address, or visit the Society's Web site at www.nationalgeographic.com.

Interior design by Michael Ian Kaye and Tuan Ching, Ogilvy & Mather, Brand Integration Group

Printed in the U.S.A.

*For Howie Michels and
Letizia Battaglia*

CONTENTS

Sicilian Odyssey

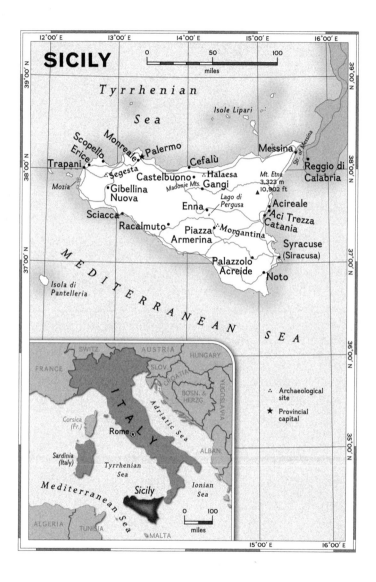

SICILY

0   50   100
miles

Tyrrhenian

Sea

Isole Lipari

Scopello
Erice
Monreale
Palermo
Messina
Str. of Messina
Trapani
Cefalù
Reggio di
Calabria
Segesta
Castelbuono
Halaesa
Mt. Etna
Mozia
Gibellina
Nuova
Madonie Mts.
Gangi
3,323 m
10,902 ft
Lago di
Pergusa
Acireale
Sciacca
Enna
Aci Trezza
Catania
Racalmuto
Piazza
Armerina
Morgantina
Syracuse
(Siracusa)
Palazzolo
Acreide
Noto

MEDITERRANEAN

Isola di
Pantelleria

SEA

SWITZ.
AUSTRIA
HUNGARY
FRANCE
SLOV.
CROATIA
BOSN. &
HERZG.
YUGOSLAVIA
Corsica
(Fr.)
ITALY
Adriatic Sea
Rome
ALBAN.
Sardinia
(Italy)
Tyrrhenian
Sea
Ionian
Sea
Sicily
Mediterranean Sea
ALGERIA
TUNISIA
MALTA

0   100
miles

∴ Archaeological
site

★ Provincial
capital

CHAPTER ONE

Arrivals

On the north coast of Sicily, which Homer called the Island of the Sun, the shipwrecked Odysseus washed up on shore and was saved by Nausicaa, the king's daughter. Farther inland, on the flowery banks of Lake Pergusa, Hades seized Persephone, the daughter of Demeter, and carried her clear across the island to a spring just south of Syracuse, where they descended into the underworld and remained there until Demeter's pleas persuaded the gods to let Persephone rejoin the living for two-thirds of every year. Pursued through Arcadia by the river god Alpheus, the nymph Arethusa prayed to Artemis for help; changed into a fountain, she reappeared across the ocean, in Syracuse, joined with her pursuer in a pool that today is overgrown with papyrus, occupied by placid white ducks, and surrounded by stylish bars. So even in pre-Homeric times it must have been

apparent that this island was so magical that the gods and heroes would naturally have come here to act out their dramas of danger and survival, of grief, mourning, and reunion.

Sicily is where Daedalus landed. After the failure of his ingenious plan to free himself and his son from King Minos's prison on the wings that he fashioned from wax, after the tragic accident he must have witnessed, watching his son soar higher and higher, closer to the sun until the wax wings melted and sent Icarus plummeting into the sea, after gathering up his son's body and burying it on the island of Icaria—only then did the architect of the Labyrinth, the inventor, and the master technician come to rest in Sicily, of all the places he could have chosen.

What did he see as he flew in and—according to the myth—touched ground somewhere along the west coast? Whatever sights greeted him would have only distantly resembled what the traveler finds today. Erice, near where Daedalus is said to have arrived, was not yet the austere and lovely medieval town swathed in mists and set high on the mountaintop like a diamond solitaire in an antique ring. The salt pans on the coast between Trapani and Marsala, the cathedral at Cefalù, the giddy baroque excesses of Noto and Palermo, the petrochemical plants at Gela—none of it would exist for centuries. Lake Pergusa—where Persephone was seized by the enamored Lord of the Underworld—had not yet been encircled by a dusty race-car track.

And the island's colorful, brutal history had not yet had a chance to cover the landscape with the rubble and dust of battle, invasion, foreign occupation, earthquakes and volcanic eruptions, warfare, tyranny, crime, and death. Inhabited by prehistoric tribes, the island had still to repel and then embrace the long succession of invaders—Greeks and Carthaginians, Romans, Goths and Vandals, Byzantines and Saracens, Normans, Swabians, the Spanish and French—all of whom would inflict great losses and bestow even greater gifts on the conquered country. In fact, the whole history of Italy—and of much of Europe—seems to have been distilled, concentrated, and acted out on this singular island. "To have seen Italy without having seen Sicily is not to have seen Italy at all," wrote Goethe, who landed in Palermo in April 1787. "For Sicily is the clue to everything."

It's easy to understand what drew the invaders here, why they bothered, what they wanted. Some part of the attraction must have been the sheer beauty, which—as Homer reminded us—men will go to extreme lengths to possess, to claim as their own. But there was also the fertility, the generosity of the soil.

From earliest times, the goddess of fertility—Cybele, Demeter, Ceres—has been worshiped here. In the archaeological museum at Syracuse is a collection of votive figurines of the goddess holding sheaves of grain. Down the hill from the Greek theater at Palazzolo Acreide are the Santoni, a dozen or so statues of Cybele roughly hewn from the rock face. The fact that the sculptures have been put behind bars—for their own protection—makes them seem all the more mysterious, otherworldly, and imposing. Every August, the hill town of Gangi decorates its streets with ears of corn tied with red ribbons—a festival that derives from the sacred rites in honor of Demeter. And in Enna, the highest major city on the island and the nearest to its geographical center, you can climb out on a rock believed to have been the most important altar in the cult of Ceres and, on rare clear days, you can see all the way to Mount Etna.

So perhaps Daedalus saw only the goddess's gifts: the golden hills, the turquoise coast, the warm sun, the stands of wild fennel and orange, and, across the island, the smoking cone of Etna with its threat or promise that something dramatic was about to happen. Perhaps he intuited or understood that he had come to a land in which the most extreme natural and man-made splendor insisted on its right to coexist with the most extreme horror, the most sustained and terrible bloodshed—a conjunction that must have seemed refreshingly truthful and even comforting in its honesty in light of the pain and loss that he had just endured. Possibly, Daedalus recognized that he had reached a place in which the most lush magnificence, the most sybaritic pleasures console us for—without ever lying about—the harshness of existence.

Rooftops, Enna

For all those reasons, it is the place where I most want to come at a time when the world has never seemed more chaotic, more savage, more precious, or more fragile. When Howie and I leave New York to spend a month in Sicily, it is February, 2002. We have not ventured very far from home since that morning last September, when, as we waited to board a plane for California at John F. Kennedy airport, we first noticed the plumes of black smoke billowing east from Lower Manhattan and joined the cluster of shocked, silent travelers gathered around a TV set. And now, like Daedalus, we have traveled to Sicily, partly to experience its mystery and fascination, the richness of its art and architecture, its history and its culture, the seamlessness with which it merges the present and the past—and partly to discover what this island has learned and can teach us about the triumph of beauty over violence, of life over death.

How strange that Daedalus should have landed in the west when, by all rights, he should have been coming from the other direction. Perhaps he had heard about—and feared—the eastern shore, the legendary Riviera dei Ciclopi, the "coast of the cyclopes," from which the blinded and infuriated Polyphemus hurled giant boulders after the fleeing Odysseus and his men. The rocks are still there, bizarrely shaped volcanic mini-islands poking out of the sea off the beach at Aci Trezza. Decorated with holy statues to bless the fishermen sailing out in their wooden boats, the islands are visible from the seafood restaurants to which chic, prosperous Catanians drive up from the city to tuck into steaming plates of linguine with lobster and *risotto alla marinara.*

Fishing boats, Aci Trezza

The Greek navigators, who first landed up the coast at Naxos, may have had good reason for steering clear of Polyphemus's stony, dangerous missiles. But for modern travelers, like ourselves, this side of the island—or more specifically, the airport at Catania—offers a gentler, more accommodating place to land than its counterpart in Palermo, with its precipitous approach and its proximity to the chaotic, homicidal traffic of the island's capital.

The plane from Rome deposits us at the sleepy Aeroporto Fontanarossa, which, in the decade since we've last been here, has come to resemble a regional airport in some distant Balkan outpost. Not that I remember precisely how things looked the last time we were here. Howie and I were traveling with my mother and our two young sons, and our most vivid memories are of yanking the boys out of the path of cars speeding in the

wrong direction up one-way streets. But we saw just enough—
and remembered enough—to have fallen in love with Sicily,
and to have promised ourselves that we would come back, as
soon as possible.

Mostly what I remembered was the beauty of its shore, its
landscape, and especially its art; and the fact that a few hours'
drive would take you from one of the world's most perfectly
preserved Greek temples to the site of the greatest surviving
Roman or Byzantine mosaics. I remember thinking that Sicily
was the place I wished I'd been born, and where I would like to
be reborn—preferably as a big, handsome, life-loving, prosperous Sicilian guy, with a large adoring family, an enormous
appetite, and no worries about weight, health, or business.
(Gender loyalty aside, I realize that being reborn as a Sicilian
woman might involve more of a daily struggle.)

Now, as I wait at the baggage carousel at the airport, I'm
surrounded by guys just like that—embracing, talking, gesturing
with their hands in semaphores so expressive of their individual
personalities, so voluble, graceful, and emphatic that it's as if
they're each conducting a symphony: the music of the language. And this—more than anything—reminds me that I'm
in Italy, in Sicily, again.

Life here burns at a high heat and lends an unusual warmth
to the people who live it. Though Sicilians have a reputation for
dourness, for severity, for short violent tempers and an agonized
religiosity, the fact is that almost every casual social interchange
we have is characterized by a remarkable sweetness. The first
policeman whom we approach to ask for directions engages us
in a fifteen-minute conversation that ranges from the annoyance

of paying high taxes to the pleasures and the relief of having (nearly) grown children. When he and Howie discover that they're the same age, they burst out laughing; each had assumed the other was years younger. A few days later, we ask a long-distance bus driver, leaving from Syracuse, how to reach the city's archaeological museum. He asks where we're from and tells us: *No problema!* Get on the bus! *"Buon giorno,* hello," he calls to the understandably startled passengers who follow us onto the bus. *"Andiamo,* get in, come on, we're going to New York!" Within minutes, he's made an unscheduled stop—a slight detour from his regular route—in order to drop us at our destination.

Much has been said and written about what the great Sicilian writer Leonardo Sciascia has called his countrymen's "natural trag-ic solitude," but what's less often remarked upon is the Sicilian sense of humor: the comedy of the puppet theater, of the folk paintings collected in Palermo's Museo Pitrè and Palazzolo Acreide's Casa Museo Uccello, of the allegorical floats of Carnival, and of the ham sandwiches and plates of spaghetti fashioned out of marzipan and displayed in the windows of the pastry shops so common that, it often seems, every city block has at least one and sometimes two *pasticcerie* or *gelaterie.* Certain sweetshops—Maria Grammatico's in Erice, for example—are known all over the island, and function as pilgrimage sites for travelers from other parts of Sicily and the mainland.

In no other region do adults have quite so fierce an ardor for pastries, candies, and ice cream; here, an ice-cream sandwich is literally an ice-cream sandwich—huge gobs of pistachio or strawberry pressed inside a brioche or a roll—and Sicilians eat them for breakfast. And like so much else about Sicily, this enthusiasm turns out to be contagious. Soon after we arrive, I find myself craving a daily cannoli and the sort of teeth-aching, sugary confections I would never dream of eating at home; just as I watch myself persuading Howie that the best way to get to our hotel is to drive—just a short distance, really—in the wrong direction up a one-way street. Still, it takes quite a while longer before I stop closing my eyes on two-lane highways when drivers cut into our lane to pass speeding trucks on inside curves at over a hundred kilometers an hour, and then dart back onto their side of the road at the very last minute, barely avoiding a head-on collision. Driving anywhere in Sicily is not for the faint of heart.

It's easy to be happy here, but it requires an adjustment that is as much biological as cultural: learning to live on Sicilian time. No one eats lunch until almost two, no one starts dinner until almost nine—the hour when the whole neighborhood goes out for pizza, which no one serves at lunch. At around one-thirty every afternoon, a kind of paradoxically high-speed gridlock seizes the roadways as everyone rushes home for lunch, shuttering stores and businesses, leaving their offices, and, within minutes, emptying the streets of the suddenly silent cities. At about seven in the evening, especially on Sundays, the local population turns out for *la passeggiata,* the slow, ritual stroll up and down the main street.

Stores are closed on Monday morning, Friday is a slow day too, and nothing at all (connected with business or commerce) happens on Sunday. Messina on a Sunday is a completely different—unrecognizable—city from the honking, buzzing madhouse that is reborn every Monday. One Sunday morning, we drive into Mazara del Vallo to find what looks like a ghost town in some postnuclear horror film. Not a soul is on the street—or anywhere, it seems. At last we walk into the Duomo, where the whole town has gathered to gossip with their friends, admire the new babies, check out the opposite sex, and pay the minimally acceptable amount of attention to the priest intoning about the importance of the catechism.

We wander outside and cross the piazza, where we find a few holdouts, mostly middle-aged and elderly men, reading the paper, smoking, chatting, and waiting for their wives and families in a kind of social club that doubles as—and that *is*, officially—a museum of ornithology. Its walls are lined with dusty glass vitrines containing dozens of stuffed birds and small forest animals baring their sharp tiny teeth in one last admirable display of ferocity, if only for the taxidermist. At last, at *long* last, the church bells ring, the townspeople come bursting out of the cathedral into the warm afternoon sunshine—and it's time for lunch.

Bleak Fontanarossa is good preparation for the suburbs of Catania, disfigured by mile after mile of the sort of dilapidated high-rise apartment buildings that evoke the grimness of Eastern-bloc state socialist housing. It's rather like an architectural memento mori. Driving past, you can't help thinking of the rubble on which it was built—founded by the Chalcidians in the eighth century B.C., Catania was destroyed by earthquakes in the twelfth and seventeenth centuries and covered by volcanic lava in 1669—and the rubble to which it is eternally in danger of returning. The outskirts form a forbidding, protective shell around the city's historical center, which for years had been steadily decaying but is at last being revitalized, thanks in part to a recent influx of technology- and computer-related industry. Catanians say that "Etna Valley" is the local equivalent of California's Silicon Valley. If the Riviera dei Ciclopi is placid and beneficent, the city of Catania—built of dark volcanic rock and cursed with a reputation for petty crime, urban neglect, and pollution—is lively, but tough in a way that demands a certain amount of vigilance and concentration.

So we have decided to base ourselves in Acireale, a half dozen or so kilometers north along the coast—a friendlier city, though it too traces its origins back to a myth of violence. In love with the nymph Galatea, the Cyclops Polyphemus grew jealous when she became enamored of the shepherd Acis, so he crushed Acis with one of his lethal boulders. The shepherd's body was divided into nine parts and scattered across the landscape, and from each part grew one of the nine towns whose names begin with Aci: Acireale, Aci Trezza, Aci Castello ...

Late on the afternoon of our arrival, we decide to go for a walk from our beachfront hotel (named, charmingly and improbably, Aloha d'Oro and built in accordance with someone's equally charming and improbable Polynesian/North African/Mexican fantasy) and to head up into town toward the Piazza del Duomo. It's misty, chilly, getting dark. But as we turn up Via Vittorio Emanuele, we begin to notice dabs of color—a baby dressed in a bright yellow bumblebee costume, a teenage boy sporting an oversize, striped-velvet, Cat-in-the-Hat stovepipe hat, a middle-aged woman in a jester's cap ringing with tiny bells. And before we know it, someone has showered us with confetti.

Shrove Tuesday is almost two weeks away, but the citizens of Acireale (home of *"il più bel Carnevale di Sicilia*—the most beautiful Carnival in Sicily") are getting a head start on their pre-Lenten celebrations. Strings of glistening lights form an arching canopy above the main streets, dance music blares out of invisible loudspeakers. In the Piazza del Duomo, the soaring, extravagantly elaborate facade of the cathedral is brilliantly illuminated, as are the stalls selling masks, roasted pumpkin seeds and chestnuts, fried sausage, panini, noisemakers, plastic bags of confetti. Half the local population—and nearly every-one under twelve—is in costume, dressed as pirates and knights, skeletons and witches; lions and lambs, angels and devils stroll hand in hand.

Some of the masks are familiar; in fact the plastic monster heads are the very same ones I saw in October, at Halloween, in New York City. And yet there's something about the spirit of the event that's entirely different from Halloween in Greenwich Village, or Mardi Gras in New Orleans, or St. Patrick's Day on Fifth Avenue. At home, public holidays have mostly become excuses for teenagers and young adults to dress up or paint their faces green and get as hammered as they'll get the following weekend, as they got the weekend before. But this pre-Carnival celebration in Acireale feels like an entirely unique moment in the yearly calendar, a time for people (many of whom clearly know one another) to step out of character, to leave their normal selves behind, and to unleash something that—precisely because of familiarity, proximity, and the need to coexist harmoniously and amicably—stays in check for the rest of the year.

To walk through Acireale in the days preceding Carnival is to understand what it means for the Lord of Misrule—that great equalizer, leveler, and liberator—to be in command. Children giddily bop their elders over the head with colorful plastic mallets that make a hollow sound somewhere between the noise of a baby rattle and the pop of a firecracker. It hurts just enough so I can feel (or think I feel) the fillings rattling lightly in my teeth, but after the first half-dozen bops, I'm no longer tempted to wheel around and show the little bopper how New Yorkers act when someone's invaded their personal space. Groups of high school students spray each other—and total strangers—with shaving cream and strings of colored foam propelled by aerosol. Shy girls clutch bags of confetti, waiting to get the nerve to fling a handful at some cute boy—for much of the revelry is energized by the explosive charge of courtship, romance, and sex.

But finally what makes the merriment seem so Sicilian is the ease with which it combines the mournful with the festive (the tunes played by the fresh-faced, earnest high school marching band are almost comically dirgelike and funereal) and the present with the past. The designs of the elaborate princess costumes (the outfit of choice for little girls) seem modeled on the gowns worn by Bourbon royalty and make their wearers look like the pretty, uncomfortable, and slightly stunned children in Velásquez's "Las Meninas." And smack in the middle of a group of kids, parading in formation and dressed like Harry Potter and his fellow students at the School for Wizards, is, incongruously, a sort of giant eyeball-on-legs meant to represent a Cyclops.

Catania's Feast of St. Agatha also takes place at the beginning of February, at the same time as the start of Acireale's Carnival, and less than ten miles away. But the atmosphere and the mood of the crowd are so remarkably different that the festival could be taking place in another country. The Feast of St. Agatha is celebratory but solemn in a way that seems appropriate for a religious holiday honoring the city's patron saint, a martyr credited with having rescued the town from an especially threatening eruption of Mount Etna; in some versions of the legend, her outstretched arms diverted a stream of lava that would otherwise have inundated the city. On cloudless days, you can see Etna's gently smoldering cone at the end of the long straight boulevard that bears its name. The last time we were in Sicily, Etna was erupting, and, from our hotel room in Taormina, we could watch the tongues of fiery orange lava snake down the mountainside.

Just before noon on the final day of the feast, a crowd of Catanians—many of whom carry long yellow candles they will light in the course of their peregrination around the holy sites associated with the saint scattered throughout the old quarter—gathers in the square in front of the stately, gloomy cathedral. The charcoal-gray volcanic rock from which so many of its buildings are constructed gives Catania the air, among Sicilian cities, of the family member with the long face, the sad story, the bad news.

At exactly twelve, a series of cannon blasts sends puffs of white smoke wafting across the blue sky; the church bells toll. And as a procession of priests, ecclesiastical dignitaries, local officials, and members of fraternal orders dressed in eighteenth-century costume emerge from the church, displaying a silver reliquary containing the relics of the saint, a young mother standing in front of me tells her small son the story of St. Agatha.

Smoothing back his hair, gently stroking his forehead, speaking in a melodious voice, she narrates a mercifully bowdlerized version—minus the gorier details—of how the blessed virgin refused to marry the suitor who had been chosen for her and, consequently, as punishment, had her breasts cut off. A visitation from St. Peter healed her wounds and restored her breasts, but Peter could not, or would not, save her from a horrible martyrdom—from the tortures that insured her beatitude and made her the patron saint of women suffering from diseases of the breast.

This evening, at the height of the festival, young men, dressed in black berets and white suits (rather like karate uniforms) and assembled in groups representing the various trade organizations, will carry the *candelore*—heavy, gilded litters decorated with images of the saint and topped with tall candles—in a procession that's part race, part endurance contest designed to see who can bear the weight longest. There will be fireworks, music, stalls selling candy, nougat, freshly made nut brittle. But beneath it all will run that Sicilian understanding that the underside of joy is grief, that the face of sacrifice and suffering is the dark mirror image of pleasure and enjoyment, that every moment of arrival is to be treasured and enjoyed in the full knowledge that it has brought us a moment closer to the moment of departure.

CHAPTER TWO

Syracuse

Sitting in the top row of the Greek amphitheater in Syracuse's
Archaeological Park, I close my eyes and try to imagine the
roar of the spectators during the city's glory days, when
Syracuse was among the most influential city-states in the
world, when its leaders could afford to build the most magnificent theaters and attract the most brilliant playwrights, when
fifteen thousand spectators crowded into these seats to watch
the tragedies of Aeschylus, who lived and worked here in the
royal court of Hiero I. What waves of excitement and anxiety
must have rippled through the crowd as the masked actors per-
formed *Prometheus Bound,* a play about the tensions between
obedience and individual freedom, between following the will
of the gods and finding the courage to break the divine law that
would have doomed mankind to live without fire, in the cold
and the darkness. How subversive—how dangerous—would

Aeschylus's words have sounded to theatergoers who lived under the rule of a greedy, violent dictator, one of the succession of tyrants who ruled Syracuse from the fifth to the second century B.C.

Like us, they believed that their civilization would last forever. Whatever they thought as they heard Prometheus cry out from the rock to which he had been chained for stealing fire from the gods and giving it to mortals, not one of them (we can only assume) could have imagined the day when, from the high rows of their theater, you could see trains in the rail yard, traffic speeding by on the highway, the tall flat roofs of the modern city built over the ruins of their own. (At the city's archaeological museum, photographs and exhibits explain exactly where excavations under the busy streets and sidewalks have exposed the remnants of ancient burial grounds.) The early Syracusans could not have foreseen this any more than Aeschylus could have anticipated that he would be killed at Gela, not far from here, when, so the story goes, an eagle dropped a tortoise directly onto his bald head, which the eagle mistook—clearly, this is one of those stories that gets progressively more implausible as you pile on the details—for the sort of rock on which it was accustomed to drop turtles, in order to smash their shells so that their insides could be eaten.

At least initially, the history of Syracuse resembled, in a general way, the history of the United States—that is, it began as a colony which became as powerful as, and then more powerful than, its mother country. The Greeks arrived in Sicily during the eighth century B.C., around the same time that Homer was dispatching Odysseus to have his adventures and misfortunes on the Island of the Sun, his travel delays and unscheduled layovers on the long journey home from Troy to Ithaca.

Establishing their first colony on the coast at Naxos, the Greek invaders quickly conquered the indigenous tribes and founded a series of outposts. Then, in the fifth century B.C., Gelon of Gela—a chariot-racing champion known for his ferocity—consolidated his power by marrying the daughter of the tyrant of Acragas (now Agrigento) and by defeating the Carthaginians at the battle of Himera. With the help of an immense Carthaginian slave-labor force captured in the war, he moved his capital from Gela to Syracuse.

There, Gelon (perhaps out of gratitude for his good fortune) began building the Temple of Athena on the island of Ortigia, which was already connected by a causeway to the mainland at Syracuse. With palm-lined boulevards bordering its shore and pink and ochre palaces giving its harbor an almost Venetian appearance, Ortigia is one of the most appealing places in all of Sicily.

In fact, when I think about being reborn as a Sicilian, it's most often in Ortigia that I imagine my new life beginning. The winding alleys are lined with abandoned baroque palazzi, many of which are in the process of being restored. Since our arrival, we have been looking longingly at the ubiquitous signs that announce *A vendersi*—FOR SALE. We fantasize about buying a derelict palace, fixing it up, persuading our friends to move into their own palazzi nearby. The light, the high ceilings, the studio space, the ocean views! As we pass one of the palaces under reconstruction, a German tourist grabs Howie's arm and pulls us over to see what he's just seen: A building site where a group of workmen digging in a basement have just discovered—and are gently unearthing—an ancient burial urn containing the bones of a child.

Gelon's temple survives on Ortigia, intact but greatly changed, its outlines and columns still visible in the walls of the Duomo. Partly what's so pleasing about the cathedral is the evidence it offers that each invader who arrived in Ortigia, each champion of each new faith, seems to have been inspired by an admirable desire to preserve and protect, rather than raze and obliterate, the remnants of the previous structure, the evidence of the old religion. In the seventh century A.D., the Doric columns of the Greek temple were incorporated by the Byzantines into the walls of a Christian church, which was in turn converted into a mosque by the Saracens, then reconsecrated by the Normans. When the facade collapsed during the earthquakes at the end of the seventeenth century, it was rebuilt according to the principles of the high baroque. This amalgamation of styles represents a heartening aspect of Sicilian history and culture—the instances in which a ruler or a people extracted what was most valuable from an older tradition; among the happy consequences are the cathedrals of Monreale and Cefalù, which combine the aesthetics of the Normans, the Byzantines, and the Arabs.

Gelon was succeeded by his brother Hiero I, the patron of Aeschylus, who was followed by another brother, Thrasybulus, one of the cruelest of the tyrants—though possibly not as vicious as the early ruler of Acragas who had his enemies roasted alive inside a specially fashioned bronze bull, the idea being that the howls of the dying would sound like the bellowing of a bull.

During the rule of Hermocrates, the quarries surrounding the amphitheater at Syracuse were first used as prisons to hold—under inhuman conditions—thousands of captives brought back from the war against Athens. (Cicero, in *The Verrine Orations,* claims the caves were employed for that purpose, though this has been disputed by some modern scholars.) In 405 B.C., the throne was assumed by Dionysius the Elder, a soi-disant poet and playwright so loutish that he had Plato imprisoned when he came to Syracuse as a guest of his brother-in-law. It was during his reign that Syracuse became one of the most powerful cities in Europe.

Dionysius was not only an effective leader but also a world-class paranoid so obsessive that he had a moat dug around his bed, complete with a drawbridge he could pull up when he went to sleep. Good fences may, as Robert Frost wrote, make good neighbors—but great paranoids make great walls. In an attempt to surround and fortify the entire settlement of Syracuse as a deterrent to foreign invasion, Dionysius built the prodigious walls of Epipolae, fragments of which can still be seen on the drive up to the ruins of the Castello Eurialo—a defensive fort strengthened by Hiero II, most likely with the help of Archimedes, and one of the largest extant examples of Greek military architecture.

The scale and ambition of the fort gives it an air of near-insanity, and indeed it's the product of a plan to encircle and protect the entire known world—the classical equivalent of the "Star Wars" missile defense shield. When you consider the amount of labor involved, the human suffering all that labor represented, and, as it turned out, the fort's utter uselessness in repelling the Roman invasion, the castello seems more aptly described as a folly than those harmless pagodas and pleasure palaces eccentric English lords built in their gardens.

And yet, for all the pointless grandiosity and wastefulness that the Castello Eurialo represents, its builder, Hiero II, was one of the more progressive and rational of the despots who ruled Syracuse. It was he who enlarged and rebuilt the amphitheater, and who built the nearby altar (also in the Archaeological Park) on which, according to Diodorus, 450 bulls were sacrificed to Zeus in a single day.

Like certain ruins—especially those in which something horrific has taken place—the Castello Eurialo retains some vestige of the spirit (in this case, of delusional mania) that inspired its construction. Bracing myself against the wind that rakes the bluff, climbing over the stone walls, exploring the grassy courtyards and the dank cells reeking of what I can only hope is mildew, I lose sight of Howie for just a few minutes and fall instantly into a sort of irrational, childish panic that feels like a combination of claustrophobia and agoraphobia, a terror of never being able to get out of, or down from, this empty, desolate, open place.

Despite the massive fortification of the Castello Eurialo and the best efforts of Archimedes, who invented a series of imaginative military gadgets (including hooks that seized and hoisted the attacking soldiers up into the air) to repel the invasion of his native city, the Romans—under the consul Marcus Claudius Marcellus—entered and destroyed much of Syracuse in 212 B.C.

Preferring blood sport to classical tragedy, the Romans modified the amphitheater, enlarging the proscenium to accommodate gladiatorial and aquatic displays and covering the front rows with marble so that the nobility could enjoy yet another advantage unavailable to the masses of ordinary theatergoers.

Not content with these relatively modest renovations, the Romans also built a huge elliptical arena for chariot races and circus games. In the center is a pool about which historians and guidebook writers disagree. Some claim it was used in the cleaning of the arena, while others speculate, more luridly, that it was intended as a receptacle for the remains of the more unfortunate participants in the Roman games, and that after the spectacles ended, the anemic and infirm would rush in to devour the internal organs of the unsuccessful athletes in the hope of benefiting from their supposed health-giving properties.

As we stand on the edge of the Roman arena, we notice, perhaps a hundred feet away and quite near the tunnel-like entrance through which the chariots used to come hurtling onto the track, an animal about which there's something so strange and uncanny that it's hard to figure out what kind of creature it is. It looks like a wolf or coyote, but in fact it's a very large and apparently feral dog, standing in a peculiar posture, leaning slightly to one side. After a moment we realize that it's nursing two puppies so big that they seem almost full-grown themselves.

I've never seen a dog stand to nurse before, let alone one suckling two such enormous pups, yet its posture seems so familiar, so ... archetypal. We both say at the same moment: Romulus and Remus. And it feels almost like a vision, a private and privileged communication from the spirit of the civilization that built this proto-speedway and then lost it first to the barbarians and then the Byzantines. The mysterious appearance of the dog and her pups seems like a gift from this city from which the Romans fled in terror, abandoning their arenas and villas and seeking refuge near Pantalica in the caves where their Bronze Age predecessors lived, two thousand years before.

Among the most celebrated visitors to Syracuse and its archaeological ruins was the painter Michelangelo Merisi, better known as Caravaggio. He arrived in 1608. Almost two years before, he had fled Rome, where he had killed a man named Ranuccio Tomassoni in a street brawl thought to have begun over a bet on a tennis game. He left the city for the surrounding countryside, then went to Naples, and then Malta, where he managed to get into even more trouble. Like so much about Caravaggio's life, the facts are unclear, but it's been suggested that he wounded yet another man in yet another fight, was imprisoned, escaped, and was wanted (and was, or so he believed, being actively pursued) by the Knights of Malta.

He was one of the era's most successful painters, but he had squandered all his money. He was known for his hot temper, his unpredictability, and for the propensity for (and fascination with) violence that underlies so much of his work, including the brutal "Beheading of St. John the Baptist," which he painted for St. John's Cathedral of Malta.

During his stay in Sicily, his behavior became progressively more erratic. He slept with a knife under his pillow and got into frequent squabbles. In Messina (where he went after

Syracuse) he allegedly slashed a painting he had just completed because he felt that his patrons' response was unacceptably tepid, and he left Messina after a fight with a local schoolmaster who insinuated that Caravaggio was hanging around the school yard and casting lecherous glances at the young male students. Working rapidly, under enormous pressure and less than optimum conditions, he nonetheless managed to produce a number of extraordinary paintings—including some of his most important masterpieces.

He had come to Syracuse partly to see an old friend and fellow painter, Mario Minniti, whom he had known in Rome. Because of Caravaggio's fame, his arrival caused considerable excitement in the city's artistic and intellectual community, and it was arranged that the celebrated archaeologist, Mirabella, would personally conduct the painter on a tour of the Greek theater and the nearby quarries.

Among the quarries, the *latomie,* that have been dug out of the hillside near the Greek theater, the most inviting and attractively landscaped is the Latomia del Paradiso, which has been turned into a park planted with orange and lemon trees, palms, and magnolias. Within its boundaries are the two most famous of the caves. The first, which has a nearly rectangular entrance, is known as the Grotta dei Cordari, the "cave of the ropemakers," most likely because its atmosphere, temperature, and humidity were perfectly suited to preserve the flexibility of the cord that the craftsmen twined into rope.

The other has a taller and more elongated mouth, a narrower, ovoid opening that rises almost toward a point; its shape suggests a cross between the spire of a cathedral and a flower in one of Georgia O'Keeffe's paintings. But what's most remark-able about this cave is its acoustical properties: When you stand in a certain spot near its entrance, you can hear your voice amplified, echoing back at you, against the choral background provided by the cooing of the pigeons that fly in and out of the cave, seemingly enjoying the music of their own voices.

The cave spirals inward, turning in on itself; at the very back is a small hole in its ceiling that, on sunny mornings, admits a single column of light, not unlike the laserlike beam that often signals the presence of the Holy Spirit shining through the window to find Mary in a Renaissance portrayal of the Annunciation. On the quiet, overcast afternoon on which we visit the quarries, one of the gardeners working in the groves of citrus trees takes us into the cave, where he whistles a bright Sicilian tune that comes bouncing back off the walls. He shows us where the light comes through and urges us to return on a clear day, when the sun will be doing its magic trick.

When Caravaggio saw the cave, he remarked that its shape resembled that of an ear, and that it was the perfect prison for a tyrant who could take advantage its acoustical properties to eavesdrop on the conversations of the captives being held there. Word of Caravaggio's observation spread rapidly through the city. A genius who so brilliantly depicted nature had instantly seen the true form and purpose of a natural wonder! No one seems to have noted the fact that a man who felt persecuted and in imminent danger of being sent to prison might natu-rally find himself thinking of incarceration, spying, etc. In any case, the cave became known—thanks to Caravaggio—as the Ear of Dionysius, a name it retains to this day, together with its reputation as a place ideally suited for the covert monitoring of its luckless inhabitants; it has also been suggested that the cave was used for less sinister purposes, to provide offstage sound effects for the nearby theater.

During his stay in Syracuse, the painter received, with Minniti's help, a desirable commission. The festival of St. Lucy, the city's patron saint, was approaching, and Caravaggio was hired to do a painting for the church believed to have been built on the site of her martyrdom. The result was "The Burial of St. Lucy," one of Caravaggio's most powerful and original works, which has been moved from its original home in the church to the city's Galleria Regionale di Palazzo Bellomo.

Nothing can prepare you for the painting's force, for the almost shocking originality of its vision and execution. It's almost unrecognizable from reproductions, which never manage to convey its prodigious scale, or the fact that nearly two-thirds of the canvas is occupied by an expanse of threatening empty space, rendered in dark earthtones and including the suggestion of a sort of grotto or cave—a void, really—not unlike the latomie the painter visited on his tour of the ruins. What's frequently reproduced is rarely the whole of the work, but rather a detail: the bottom third of the painting.

The entire action—the narrative, such as it is—transpires in that lower third, where the burial is in progress. It takes a moment to locate the figures amid all that darkness, and a moment more to find the holy martyr, who is nearly hidden from the viewer.

You have to search for the saint, the nominal subject of the painting. Because what you see first—what you can't help seeing first—are the two gravediggers, one of whom has his broad, muscular back turned toward you. Only when you've looked past and around the vitality of their bodies, the luminescence of the drapery pulled diagonally across the massive buttocks of the gravedigger on the right, past the hard, brutish labor in which they are engaged—they might as well be human backhoes—only then do you see the martyred virgin, enclosed by a small circle of church officials, onlookers, and mourners, one of whom, a grief-stricken old woman, covers her face with her hands. (Like "The Crucifixion of St. Peter" in Rome, the painting reveals Caravaggio's continuing fascination with those who did the physical work—the stoop labor—of the sacred event.)

Fragile and pale, her lips slightly parted, lying directly on the ground, the saint (whose throat was more raggedly slashed in an earlier version of the painting, which Caravaggio modified) seems already to have become another sort of being, to belong to a whole other species than the living men and women who surround her with their harsh exertions and their painful, raw emotions. Shining from some untraceable, unidentifiable source, the light catches and plays on her upturned chin and her delicate, girlish shoulder. Everything seems to have been painted in haste (as no doubt it was), with terrific urgency and intensity. The feet of the gravediggers are sketched in, roughly indicated but unfinished, as if the artist had no interest in—no time for—such irrelevant details, though it's also possible that this section may have been the most heavily damaged during the centuries in which the work fell into disrepair.

In any case, what's most striking and most unique—and what can most easily be appreciated if you compare the painting with the far more staid and conventional portrayal of the martyrdom of St. Lucy, by Caravaggio's friend Minniti, which is also in the museum—is what's missing, what Caravaggio has willfully, unconsciously, or instinctively chosen to leave out, to withhold. In Minniti's rendering, both the virgin and her killer, whose knife is pointed menacingly at her throat, stare at us out of the picture; what it offers, as Caravaggio's does not, is a sense of a theatrical performance being staged for the viewer, played out with the audience in mind.

By contrast, there is nothing that includes you, or invites you, into Caravaggio's rendering; indeed, the gravediggers are doing everything possible to keep you at a distance, to conceal the tragic scene from view—just as, in life, the participants in something sorrowful, violent, and shameful might try to keep it secret, hidden. What's even more striking is all that earth, all that brown, all that darkness taking up all that room in the painting. There are no clouds here, no starry firmament, no heaven, no promise of ascension, no vision of an afterlife surrounded by plump, pink-cheeked cherubs and choirs of angels. There is only earth, only darkness, only the fierce and brutal energies of the living. That, Caravaggio seems to be saying, is all there is.

It is perhaps the darkest and certainly among the most hopeless and least consoling of religious paintings. Yet there is something profoundly comforting about its honesty, its bravery, its conviction—and, above all, in the depth and beauty that Caravaggio has managed to wrest from this scene of mourning and almost unmediated pain.

The danger and seduction of retrospect lie in how much we try to read back into the events that preceded what would ultimately reveal itself as the future. Looking at "The Burial of St. Lucy," we not only find ourselves assuming that its dark vision must have been influenced by the misfortune and violence that Caravaggio had already experienced, but we may also be tempted to find some ominous presentiment of how little time the painter had left and of the misery that lay before him.

Leaving Syracuse, Caravaggio continued on to Messina, and then to Palermo, all the while painting furiously, taking on local commissions and smaller paintings that he hoped to bring to his patrons in Rome, partly in the hopes that his new works would move them to intercede for him and obtain a pardon that would allow him to return safely home. When this began to seem probable, he left Sicily for a brief sojourn in Naples, where he was gravely wounded and disfigured in another fight. Then, bringing along several paintings, he set sail for Rome.

His boat stopped at Porto Ercole, and, possibly mistaken for someone else, he was detained and imprisoned. While he was being questioned by the authorities, the tides shifted, and it was necessary for the boat to leave.

Impatient, enraged to find himself stranded in the port, Caravaggio set off for the capital on foot, a dangerous hike through swamps infested with malaria, which (or so it is thought) the painter contracted, and from which he is believed to have died, en route to Rome. Like so much about his life, his death remains shrouded in uncertainty. All that we know is that his last great paintings continued on their sea journey and arrived safely in Rome, without him.

CHAPTER THREE

Building and Rebuilding:
the Glories of the Baroque

For many years, when we lived in rural upstate New York, one of our neighbors was a carpenter-contractor who had a placard in his front yard advertising his business: BUILDING AND REBUILDING. We used to think the sign was funny, sort of, as if it described an ongoing process, a series of events that amounted to a confession of incompetence. First he would build and later, by necessity, rebuild what he'd screwed up the first time.

Here in Sicily, I keep thinking of him and of his sign, which, oddly, has begun to seem like a terse summary of the energies, the aims, the history of the Sicilian baroque—so much of which involved a series of reconstructions and revisions, powered by disturbing memories of the destructive powers of time and nature, and by a brighter notion of a future in which the forces of devastation and ruin could be overcome, or at least temporarily subdued.

Throughout Sicily, especially in Palermo and in the southeast, the baroque seems always to be waiting just around the corner, positioned in the exact place where the sun is most likely to strike it and produce the maximum brilliance, the optimum dazzle. Travel up a narrow, dark, cobblestone medieval street in a remote hill town and, suddenly, you're standing in a spacious, open piazza, where the scale expands to confront you with the scrollwork, the curlicues, the heroic staircase of a church, its stone facade perfectly sited to catch the golden rays and reflect them back at the few elderly worshipers arriving for morning Mass. Pause in the midst of an undistinguished alley and look up, and all at once you're staring at the underside of a balcony, decorated with gargoyles, chimeras, coiled serpents—architectural elements with no sensible justification, no other purpose than adornment.

Yet often these optimistic, exuberant buildings and extravagant details are in advanced states of disrepair, propped up by scaffolding, awaiting the influx of money and energy necessary to restore them to their former splendor. Nowhere is this more obvious, more thought provoking—or more heartbreaking—than in the town of Noto, in the southeast corner of Sicily, an hour or so from Syracuse. If Noto is the island's most famous baroque city, it's because it represents a sustained and conscious experiment in the baroque, the attempt to construct a designed and planned community (think of the eighteenth-century equivalent of Celebration, Florida) that—like so many such experiments—has, over time, made the sobering discovery that God and nature had entirely different plans for it.

Originally located a few miles away, at a site now known as Noto Antica, Noto was destroyed completely in the cataclysmic earthquake of January 1693. Sad experience and sustained government pressure persuaded the city fathers (who at first wanted to reconstruct their home on the ruins of the old settlement) that its former location was too vulnerable, and so it was decided to rebuild the town in its current spot.

Inspired by this opportunity for renewal, and mostly financed by the Spanish government, construction was begun, directed by the Duke of Camastra, who had already demonstrated his urban planning abilities at Santo Stefano di Camastra. Sicily's greatest architects—among them Vincenzo Sinatra, Paolo Labisi, and Rosario Gagliardi, a disciple of Borromini—were brought in to collaborate on the project that was conceived as an opportunity to apply the essential principles and to realize the aims of the baroque aesthetic: an amalgam of rationality and grotesquerie, order and dynamism, capricious wit and grand theatricality.

Local craftsmen were employed to decorate the elaborate palazzi and construct the sweeping staircase of the cathedral, as well as the Convento del Santissimo Salvatore and the Chiesa di San Francesco. Plasterers were set to work, layering decorative moldings and squadrons of winged putti on the church interiors. Altars were constructed of multicolored marble, inlaid in intricate patterns. And the city was separated into quarters according to the intended purpose—ecclesiastical, residential, commercial—of each neighborhood and the social class of its inhabitants.

San Francisco all'Immacolata, Noto

Everywhere, you can see evidence of the optimism of this project, of the belief that nature could—by employing a precisely calibrated chemistry of scientific engineering, wishful thinking, and sheer defiance—be prevented from repeating the ravages and cruelties of the past. Nowhere is this more obvious than in the Palazzo Villadorata, a fanciful confectionery of stonework depicting yearning mermaids, charging horses, griffins, monsters, and clownish faces whose expressions are impossible to read. Are they knowing or foolish, ironic or half-crazed, and whom, exactly, are they mocking?

Perhaps they are laughing at their creators, whose ambitions for the city have been, more than three centuries later, mostly undone. In its excessiveness, its overrichness, its imaginativeness, and its less easily definable quality of flying in the face of good taste, practicality, and common sense, the palace may remind you of the candies and cream pastries in the *pasticcerie* found all over the island, and of which there are several famous examples in Noto. What the Palazzo Villadorata and the bargelateria Corrado Costanzo have in common is a faith in pleasure for its own sake, regardless and in spite of what we know about what's reasonable, what's good for our health, what will prolong our lives and protect us.

In the mid-1980s, it was discovered that even a slight tremor of the Earth could cause damage severe enough to approach the horrors of the catastrophe of 1693. Emergency repairs were begun, and over the next few years, cars—whose exhaust and vibrations had undermined the stability of the weakened structures—were banned from the town center. Even so, the great dome of the cathedral collapsed during a thunderstorm in 1996, and it is presently being restored behind a curtain hung over the scaffolding and painted to show the face of the cathedral in happier, healthier days.

Indeed, nearly everything in Noto is under construction or awaiting reconstruction, building or rebuilding. Like exoskeletons, steel braces keep the damaged facades from buckling and collapsing. There are cracks in the interior walls of the church, iron cables buttress sagging arches, metal plates cover the exteriors in an effort to stave off their disintegration. Though travel guides and art books still refer to Noto as a jewel of the baroque—a showpiece of golden sandstone eloquently testifying to its creators' fascination with views, perspective, harmony, and symmetry—the truth is altogether different. The chasm between the optimism of the baroque, the hope and humor that you can still read in the extant glories of Noto, and the experience of being in the contemporary town is something like the contrast between the extravagantly overdecorated churches of Palermo and the reliquaries displaying fragments of bone and rotten cloth, housed under the altars of the rococo chapels.

Present-day Noto is a shadow of its former self, a scrim much like the one that covers the Duomo and beneath which you can just perceive the outlines of what it must once have been. And its citizens seem to know that their town is approaching—or, one hopes, rebounding from—a low point in the cycle of collapse and construction, of design and decay, of building and rebuilding. The population is mostly geriatric, and on a weekday morning the town's young men stand along the sidewalks, loafing and chatting—not working. People know you're not from here, and make no secret of their low-level curiosity and even lower-level resentment. It's not a particularly comfortable or inviting place to be; the residents seem aware of the fact that though plenty of tourists, art lovers, and students of the baroque traipse regularly through their town, they don't spend much money—or do much to pump up the local economy—in the handful of souvenir shops and the few simple restaurants and hotels.

The stories you hear about rural Sicily, about the country villages in which, as in certain vintage Westerns, a stranger's arrival is greeted by the shuttering of windows, the slamming of doors, and the ominous, sudden disappearance of the entire population, all of that comes back to you as you walk through Noto. But whatever fears and suspicions those stories represent don't seem to apply here, exactly. What you mostly fear, in

Noto, is that a chunk of elegant baroque masonry will finally dislodge itself, fall, and land on your head.

And yet, and yet ... to truly appreciate the beauty and brilliance of Noto, its originality and inventiveness and optimism, to see it anew as if each gargoyle and fillip of scrollwork were still bright, pristine, and freshly minted, you need only spend an hour (or as much as you can bear) in Noto's modern equivalent: Gibellina Nuova.

In January 1968 a violent earthquake destroyed a major section of south-central Sicily. The farming town of Gibellina—not far from Salemi and Castelvetrano—was leveled; the only thing that survived, more or less intact, was its cemetery. Inspired perhaps by the example of Noto, the town decided to rebuild a few kilometers away, in a less perilous spot. And that's where the resemblance to Noto ends.

Gibellina Nuova is one of the creepier and more disturbing places in Sicily, and (at least in terms of architecture and urban planning) possibly anywhere I know. Artists from all over the island were enlisted to help with the project, but you can't help wondering how much control or influence they actually had. Throughout the modern town, examples of dated and sadly misdirected 1970s public sculpture pop up from the lunar landscape in varying states of neglect and disrepair. Yet their condition is shipshape compared to that of the city itself.

The marble sidewalks of the deserted main square are chipped and broken, metal reinforcement rods poke through the surface of half-poured concrete, everywhere are unfinished building projects, though often it's hard to tell what's still being constructed and what's already falling apart; much of Gibellina Nuova seems to have met—and got stuck—somewhere in the middle. The streets are depopulated and bare, like those of certain California suburbs; you can drive through them easily enough, but you wouldn't want to walk.

Perhaps what makes Gibellina so alarming—and so notably un-Sicilian—is that the past seems to have been wholly obliterated, swallowed and erased along with the original town. For though Sicily is thoroughly modern, in some ways more so than the mainland—tiny country inns and rural *agroturismo* farms all seem to have their own Web sites, a surprising number of restaurants and public spaces practice a strict no-smoking policy, you actually see people jogging—the past is always imminent, and the centuries have, by necessity, learned to coexist.

It's more than just a matter of architecture, of the church built on top of the Greek temple, the baroque palazzo standing beside the Bauhaus-inspired office complex. The interaction of past and present affects, for better and worse, the way people live their lives, from the large institutions (the church and the family still exert enormous influence over the culture) to the minutiae of daily existence, so that it's not uncommon, in the countryside, to see drivers chatting on their cell phones as they wait for herds of sheep to cross the road. Especially in rural Sicily, the average citizen's ability to get a job, to find housing, to arrange for the simplest necessities, depends on history, on connections—on who your family is and was, on what transpired generations ago between your ancestors and the ancestors of the boss you are asking for employment.

But in Gibellina, there is no visible sign of the past, or perhaps the problem is that there *is* no progress, no viable present, no future, and so everything has remained locked in the past—frozen in some deranged version of the 1970s. Judged by the standards of a more typical Sicilian town, everything seems severely dysfunctional; no one gathers to chat in the piazza, and the market suggests those bleak, transient Gypsy encampments on the edges of housing blocks in northern Italian industrial cities.

To be fair, few towns are recognizable from their descriptions in tourist brochures, but the language of the pamphlet I get from the helpful but understandably suspicious fellow (what, he obviously wonders, are we *doing* here, taking pictures?) in the underfurnished information office seems particularly inapplicable: "The New Gibellina ... shows an urban structure characterized by the alternation of pedestrian precincts and carriageways, each with a small garden. Sculptures of great contemporary artists have been located, little by little, in the wide spaces of urban territory."

If Noto Antica is a romantic spot containing a few stones and relics mostly covered over by greenery, moss and creeping vines, nature has been effectively prevented from reclaiming the site of the original Gibellina by Alberto Burri, a well-known and otherwise gifted artist, who has been covering the remains (the *ruderi*) of the medieval town with a layer of poured concrete—120,000 square meters scored with crevasses to mark where the streets used to be. Up close and from a distance, the piece, entitled "Il Cretto," suggests a giant concrete bandage applied to a wound that will never be allowed to heal, or at least not until the earthwork/memorial follows the road to ruin that Gibellina Nuova seems to be taking.

Rumor has it that the funds allocated for the rebuilding of Gibellina attracted a considerable amount of Mafia attention, and that Mafia-related graft and corner-cutting is responsible for the shoddy quality of the construction and its consequent decay. The Mafia's passionate interest in the building trades is the partial subject of *The Day of the Owl,* one of Leonardo Sciascia's most well-known novels. And many Sicilians say that while the Mafia's bloodlust—the killings and assassinations—has declined in recent years, its enthusiasm for lucrative, shoddy, and bogus public-works projects has grown even more intense. It's hard, otherwise, to explain this second tragedy to have afflicted Gibellina except to blame it on the (one assumes) highly unusual and definitely infelicitous marriage between Mafia corruption and hideous '70s art. The result makes the loneliest, most haunted de Chirico painting look like one of those cheerful small-town dreamscapes painted by Norman Rockwell.

CHAPTER FOUR

In Acireale, some of the baroque palazzi are also under scaffolding, but here, in contrast to Noto, you feel that the
rebuilding and reconstruction might actually be completed
some day. It also seems possible that the remodeling might be
cosmetic rather than structural—just a bit of last-minute
sprucing up to get Acireale ready for "Sicily's most beautiful
Carnival." During the ten days or so that the Carnival celebrations have been in progress—days we've spent in Syracuse and
Noto—no one's energy seems to have diminished in the slightest.
On this sunny late afternoon, as costumed kids and grown-ups
trickle into town for the daily parade of the *"gruppi mascherati e
folkloristi,"* it's obvious—in case it was ever in doubt—that
Sicilians know how to party.

The stars of the afternoon's event are O Revotapopolo,
a band composed of musicians of all ages, dressed in maroon-

Carnival, Acireale

and-yellow outfits and comical hats, led by a curly-haired, middle-aged maestro in a top hat and tails, brandishing a staff and displaying an air of madcap insouciance thinly overlying a no-nonsense determination that emerges when he wants to get his players off their cell phones—their *telefonini*—and in formation, out on the street.

The music starts up, a tarantella that segues into a zippy version of the Macarena, the Habanera, the Guantanamera, and back to a series of Sicilian folk tunes that the crowd seems to know. Soon everybody is bouncing in place and swaying back and forth; three grandmothers in fur coats begin to dance, bending their knees and shaking their arms in a sort of samba they're inventing on the spot.

The band's got a strange instrumentation. In addition to the saxophones, trumpets, and trombones, one young man plays rhythm on a contraption made from a mouthpiece and a long pipe attached to a chamber pot, while others mark time with clappers in the shape of scissors and brightly painted wooden violins that turn out to be percussion instruments. Everybody's having a fabulous time, and it's all hilarious—especially since several band members play no music at all but have been assigned the task of clowning, running around among the rows of musicians with animated gadgets strapped to their backs.

One of these mechanisms features a girl doll and a boy doll attached to a string that makes the boy doll appear to periodically hike up the girl doll's skirt. My favorite performer is a kid of maybe fourteen or fifteen, wearing glasses and, attached to his back, a toilet with a sign that says OCCUPATO. At regular intervals—in time to the music, in fact—the lids on the bowl and the tank lift simultaneously, and two costumed dolls pop out. The kid—you've seen his type before, he's the class clown, the joker, the funny kid from a Fellini movie—is having such a marvelous time he's nearly demented with joy. The other musicians and the spectators love him; whatever he's doing is working, he and his animated toilet are a huge success.

Over the loudspeaker, the voice of the master of ceremonies redirects our attention to a different part of the square, where another brass band strikes up still more folk tunes. These musicians, all wearing bright wigs and clown costumes, follow somewhat dutifully behind a group of high school girls dancing in formation and waving pom-poms. The girls' short, striped satin costumes—outfits that seem modeled on some murky memory or fantasy of Carmen Miranda—gleam in the afternoon sun. The announcer explains that the dancers have adopted a Brazilian theme in honor of Carnival and in solidarity with the Brazilian group that has been invited to perform for the festival and that will soon be appearing in the square.

But the girls don't look Brazilian at all, they look like Sicilian high school kids, modest and excruciatingly self-conscious, alternately shaking their hips and stopping to pull their blouses down over the gaps that reveal bare midriffs and rolls of baby fat. When they're obliged to cede the spotlight to another band, the girls seem relieved, though later in the evening, when I again see them performing, they've gotten looser, more relaxed. Perhaps the gathering darkness has given them some cover under which they feel freer to express the Brazilian abandon that seems at once expected of and forbidden them.

Meanwhile, other bands of masked revelers have begun moving slowly down the *corso*. Harry Potter and his student wizards are back, waving their straw brooms and twirling in their heavy academic robes and pointed witches' hats. The Norman knights engage in casual, balletic sword fights with little boys in the crowd, who are also wearing medieval costumes and brandishing swords of their own. An old man dressed as Geppetto the shoemaker performs a strange mini-drama of adoration and heartbreak in front of a human-size marionette of Pinocchio.

Yet another group acts out the story of Acis and Galatea, with the title roles played by two costumed teens who appear to be lovers in real life; I saw them kissing before the parade began. The ill-starred shepherd and his nymph are followed by a hulking cave man with a club and a single eye in the middle of his forehead, clearly meant to represent the jealous, vengeful Cyclops but looking more like Fred Flintstone on steroids. Ahead of this goofy trio march some girls dressed in blue, rippling streamers of azure satin symbolizing the sea, and behind them some boys in kelly green, whose symbolic function is less clear (are they earth spirits, maybe?) and who, in any case, are less interested in getting with the mythological program than they are in bopping along to the music and punching each other in the back.

Suddenly, the mood of the crowd shifts; you can feel it in the air. And the announcer introduces the *real* Brazilians, a samba group from Rio who have been performing at Carnivals up and down the Ionian coast and are now appearing in *our own Acireale.* A brace of drummers play a thrumming African beat that cuts like a knife through the bouncy rhythms of the Sicilian folk tunes, and the brass bands fall silent.

A hush falls over the crowd as twenty or so dancers appear. Their skin ranges in color from ebony to coffee to white, and they're showing a lot of it. In fact, most are nearly naked, wearing only sequined bras, G-strings, and feathered headdresses.

The troupe from Rio includes a few men, but the majority of the dancers are female—or are they? Some look like women, others appear to be transsexuals in various stages of the sex change process, some further along than the rest. Anyway, they're all convincing enough so that it takes me a while to sort out their gender identities, or—more accurately— to admit that I'll never be able to sort them out. And I can't help wondering how much (or any) of this the Sicilian grandmas are getting.

Certainly the question occurs to the people who have chosen to watch the parade, broadcast live, on a large-screen television in a pizzeria a block or so off the corso. They watch in silence, forgetting their steaming slices of fresh *porcini* pizza, as the camera zooms in on the faces of the dancers and splices live performance footage from the piazza with recorded studio interviews that the Brazilians gave earlier, "conversations" that mostly involve the dancers advancing menacingly on the cameras and shouting out their names.

What all the Brazilians appear to share in common is an unusually high level of sexual confidence and (despite, or because of, their gender ambiguity) a hearty dose of aggression about their sexuality. In that way, they remind me of the bands of eunuchs I've seen in India: Begging, dancing, singing in the streets, the eunuchs are absolutely and unabashedly in your face with their sexual outlaw status. And in Acireale's Piazza del Duomo, the Brazilians make you realize, by contrast, how traditional and old-fashioned gender roles still remain, for the most part, in provincial Sicily. Except for one female trumpet player in a sequined bowler hat, all the Sicilian musicians are male, while the pom-pom girls and majorettes are working overtime to seem coquettish and demonstrably nubile.

As the drums get louder, the Brazilians dance up a storm. Though they smile and playfully interact with their audience, no one runs around this little group with noisemaking chamber pots and animated toilet bowls. There's nothing relaxed, ironic, or self-mocking here, their brand of sex is serious business.

Unlike the other musical groups, the Brazilians are surrounded by uniformed representatives of the city's Carnival

At the Carnival, Acireale

committee, hustling alongside the performers, running interference between them and the crowd, and barking into their walkie-talkies; on their faces are the grimaces of tension, concentration, and responsibility you see on Secret Service agents protecting government officials. And in fact the guards' presence seems necessary. The Brazilians are putting out a strange vibe, it's as if they're tempting, taunting the crowd to rush them, to come and touch their bare skins, to see if they are real. The force field surrounding them could hardly be more unlike that which emanates from the goofy, good-humored brass bands.

I'm so enthralled by the Brazilians that I'm startled when I turn and notice that the gigantic illuminated floats for which the Carnival in Acireale is famous have been lit up and have begun to drift down the street. Rainbow-colored, grotesque, tall enough (and ingeniously designed) so that the figures on them can bend to fit under the telephone and electrical wires, most of the floats are, essentially, enormous political cartoons. One portrays Prime Minister Berlusconi riding on "the rooster that laid a golden egg." Another features the Italian cultural heroes whose faces used to appear on lire notes and who have now been rendered "homeless" by the adoption of the euro. Yet another, "Homage to the 20th Century," is covered by cartoon versions of "geniuses": Picasso, Mahatma Gandhi, Chairman Mao, Laurel and Hardy, Einstein, Lenin, Charlie Chaplin, and Yasir Arafat.

But it's the last float—the smallest, the only one covered by flowers, by maroon and yellow carnations—that's the most amazing.

Rearing up from the center of the float is a dragon with wild, rolling eyes, a jaw that clamps open and shut revealing curved pointed teeth, and huge claws with curved pointed nails. In front of the monster is a heart in which a young girl perches, dressed in white and wearing a spiked crown. She's meant to represent Lady Liberty, but she looks more as if she's taking her first Communion or playing the Virgin in a grade-school Christmas pageant.

On either side of the dragon is a demon, with a rocket engine on its back, wearing an old-fashioned aviator's helmet, and with its dark pink tongue protruding. And behind the monster are the giant, unmistakable representations of the World Trade towers, tilted at giddy angles, like the antic, anthropomorphic, loony-tune structures with which Red Grooms used to decorate his installations, his homages to New York.

Two airplanes, fuchsia-colored, plow into the towers. Lights shine from the skyscrapers' windows, and, at intervals,

Carnival float, Acireale

Carnival, Acireale

the top of one of the buildings collapses down onto itself, reducing the structure to half its size. Between the towers, also covered in yellow flowers, is a gigantic representation of the head of the Statue of Liberty. The dove of peace flies off to one side, while, near the front of the float, an American flag hangs from a beam until it becomes so covered in the shaving cream and party foam the onlookers are spraying that someone thoughtfully takes it down. Meanwhile, two young women dressed as New York City firefighters (in helmets and protective gear, dark heavy jackets and trousers banded with stripes of glow-in-the-dark yellow) dance distractedly to the loud, repetitive techno music that blares from the speakers.

It's all so beautiful and so incredibly tasteless, so misguided and so heartfelt. It represents such a deep outpouring of sympathy and such a profound expression of the belief that life must go on (which is what the Sicilians have been saying to me as soon as they learn where we come from and that our house is only a short distance from the World Trade Center) and of the profound conviction that some humor and brightness, vitality and even joy must be found even in the most terrible tragedy. It reminds me of the comical skeleton figures with which Mexicans mark the Day of the Dead: There's that same acknowledgment of the fact that death is so powerful, so unspeakably cruel that, at times, tears seem somehow beside the point, there's nothing to do but laugh. The Sicilians know how to celebrate, and they know how to mourn, and they know how to do both at nearly the same time.

Still, it's clear that most of the Sicilians around me have no idea what to make of the float, not a clue as to how they should be reacting. And like them, I feel overwhelmed by the float's grandeur, its scale, and above all by its (to say the least) problematic approach to its disturbing subject matter. Yet if the crowd seems a little uncertain about the correct response, I seem to be the only one who reacts without thinking, the only one with tears welling up in my eyes.

It's chilly in the piazza, night's come—somehow I hadn't noticed how dark and cold it was till now. And it strikes me: I want a drink. Howie and I duck into a nearby café and, surrounded by Sicilian families, we sit across from a little girl dressed as a pussycat and slowly working over her ice cream, eating every last drop with rapt, transfixed fascination. We order grappas and drink them, too fast, the moment they arrive.

CHAPTER FIVE

I Mosaici

In the Villa Romana del Casale, the fourth-century Roman mansion decorated with the most extensive mosaics to have survived the destruction of the empire, the Cyclops depicted on the floor of the Vestibule of Polyphemus has three eyes. Two regular eyes, normally set, and another, smack in the middle of his forehead, give a wistful, puzzled look to the traditionally one-eyed monster, who sits amid his flock of sheep, with a slaughtered, half-eviscerated ram across his lap, preparing to devour it raw. Beside him stand Odysseus and his men, offering the Cyclops the chalice of wine that will, they hope, get him drunk enough so that they can escape from his lair. Behind him is the mouth of his cave and, behind that, the cone of Mount Etna.

Perhaps the master craftsmen—mosaicists believed to have been brought in from North Africa—got that part of the story wrong, the detail about the number of eyes. In which case, it's daunting to imagine the wrath of their supervisor, who appeared at the end of the day to check on the progress of the work and noticed ... Or perhaps it was intentional, perhaps one eye just didn't seem enough amid all that decorative splendor, all that show of wealth and skill and state-of-the-art architectural design employed in the construction of the villa thought to have belonged to Emperor Maximian, who ruled the empire along with Diocletian, and who used the estate as his summer pleasure palace. Later, after Maximian was deposed from the imperial throne, his country house became the retreat where he plotted his return to power.

Like the Teatro Greco in Syracuse, the Villa Romana del Casale near the city of Piazza Armerina is the product of a culture that was blissfully unable to see the writing on the wall. Unlike the Norman palaces scattered throughout most of the island—thickly walled structures that reflect the concerns of a society based on insecurity, on semiconstant warfare, and a continual awareness of the need for protection and fortification—the Roman villa gives no indication that its inhabitants believed they would be called upon to do much more than take hot and cold baths, rub themselves (or have themselves rubbed, by servants) with perfumed oils, exercise, play games, listen to music, have love affairs, hunt, and fish.

And the floors on which they walked were meant to portray the lives they lived and wished to continue living, and which they believed would continue uninterrupted despite the fact that the empire was already showing fault lines, suffering from internal and external pressures—the strains and tensions that would soon pull it apart. Meanwhile, the Romans continued to exploit the country around them, to practice the system of latifundia (estates owned largely by absentee landlords who extracted every bit of wealth from their holdings without much caring about the fates of the people who lived and worked there) that would continue, in one form or another, throughout much of Sicily's history and accelerate the economic decline that would affect the island for centuries afterward.

But the Villa Romana is not a place in which people seem to have thought much about the future; they were too busy celebrating the delights of the present moment and the glories of a mythological past. In one room, the charming so-called Bikini Girls—dressed appropriately for exercise, in their underwear—toss a ball around, work out with weights and a discus, and crown each other for their skill in gymnastics. In a nearby antechamber, the emperor's wife and children are surrounded by servants bearing bolts of cloth and boxes of perfumed oils. There's a scene of seafaring cherubs sporting with dolphins, another of two lovers embracing. In the Sala della Danza, a young woman dances while twirling a veil above her head, while in the Sala del Circo, riders compete in a chariot race held in honor of Demeter, probably much like the ones staged in the arena at Syracuse.

But by far the most sophisticated and dynamic scenarios—the ones that most clearly engaged the energy and expertise of the artists and artisans—portray blood sports and struggles to the death, the hostile and combative relationships between the fiercest and most helpless members of the animal kingdom. Perhaps in honor of the fact that Maximian took the surname

Part of the Great Hunt mosaic, Villa Romana del Casale, Piazza Armerina

Herculius and adopted the Greek hero as the equivalent of a household god, the mosaics in the triclinium illustrate the labors of Hercules. In one area the mythic hero has shot his poisoned arrows into the prodigiously overdeveloped chests of the Titans, whose writhings are accentuated by the fact that their legs turn into the tails of serpents. Elsewhere he defeats a sea monster threatening a maiden and carries off the sacred oxen of Geryon.

Still, all of Hercules's most brutal and strenuous labors seem controlled and highly civilized compared to the scenes that illuminate the Room of the Small Hunt and the Corridor of the Great Hunt—the largest and most famous room in the villa. Everywhere you look, someone or something is killing or being killed. Leopards pounce and sink their teeth into the backs of harts. Hunters stick wild boars with spears and chase terrified deer into huge nets. No species is exempt from pain and suffering.

One man beats another with a stick, another is being viciously attacked by an enraged lioness, while in one of the more disturbing and enigmatic scenes, a griffin carries in its claws a box with slats through which we can see the head of a boy.

What's on view in the monumental corridor is not an amusing hunting party, our gracious host and a few friends riding out for a day of sport in the neighborhood around the villa. It's a big-game hunt, in Africa, and across the bottom of the mosaic is an unmistakable representation of the quarry that's being stalked. Men are loading an elephant, and antelope, and an exotic bird (on ostrich, perhaps) into a boat that will bring them back to Europe to be exhibited in zoos and killed at the hunting games held for public entertainment in the arenas. Meanwhile, a merchant coolly discusses the transport and the price he will receive for the captured beasts. And what are we supposed to make of the fact that this portrayal of the plunder of Africa was most likely done by artists who had themselves been imported from Africa to decorate the mansion of Emperor Maximian?

It keeps reminding me of another palace belonging to another aristocrat: Konopiste, the former home (in what is now the Czech Republic) of Archduke Francis Ferdinand, another near-maniacal hunting enthusiast, who filled his sporting lodge with thousands of trophies, from bear skins to fans made from the feathers of small birds he'd blown to smithereens with cannon. Like Maximian, who was killed in 310 in his struggle to regain power, Francis Ferdinand would himself die violently, assassinated at Sarajevo. And like Maximian—whose son Maxentius died in a battle with Constantine, who then took over the Villa Romana—Francis Ferdinand would continue to cause more havoc and bloodshed, even after death.

The other thing I can't seem to get out of my mind is something I saw just this morning as we drove across the fertile and mostly unpopulated plain of Catania, which the Greeks called the land of the Laestrygonians after the race of cannibals that they believed inhabited the area. For the first twenty miles or so outside of Catania, at the juncture where each country lane and dirt road met the main highway, a young African woman, nicely dressed and wearing heavy makeup, sat, dispiritedly, on a chair or crate, awaiting customers. They were prostitutes, brought there largely to service the truck drivers plying the long-distance routes across the island.

I keep recalling their sad, haunted faces as I see the mosaic depiction of an obviously venerable tradition: the importation and exploitation of Africa for the enjoyment and entertainment of Europe.

Travel through Sicily is filled with such moments, instances when the curtain of the present parts to reveal a connection, a parallel to something that occurred thousands of years before. Mostly, such moments are pleasant. In Cefalù's Museo Mandralisca is a Greek vase from the fourth century B.C. depicting a tuna vendor slicing off a chunk of a prodigious fish to sell to a skeptical customer—an eerily accurate depiction of a scene I saw just a week before, in the fish market at Catania. From the ruins of Halaesa, the site of a community of Sicels, Sicily's original inhabitants, you can watch workers tunneling under the mountains to build the new autostrada between Palermo and Messina—the modern equivalent of the engineering feat required to build, on a mountaintop, a once-great city like Halaesa.

Founded around 40 B.C., Halaesa reached the height of its glory during the first century A.D., when its wealth attracted the unwanted attentions of the rapacious tax collector, Verres, whose crimes Cicero was sent to investigate; subsequently a series of unfair and destructive levies caused the city to decline. (In Enna, a plaque marks the spot where Cicero stayed on his mission to protect Sicily from its would-be exploiter.) And the parallels go deeper; though the building of the new autostrada facing Halaesa may be completely accountable and honest, it's well known that, for decades, the Mafia has managed to collect a considerable share of the funding for highway construction and similar "improvements" on the island's infrastructure.

But surely such disturbing parallels—the link between the African prostitutes on the plains of Catania and the majestic creatures whose kidnapping from their African homes is documented by the mosaics of Piazza Armerina—are warnings against being too thoroughly beguiled by the island's scenic wonders, too easily charmed and deceived by its romantic allure. Later on the same day that we spend at the Villa Romana, we visit the ruins of Morgantina, a town first inhabited during the Bronze Age, thirteen hundred years before Christ, then later settled by the Sicels and destroyed most probably by Ducetius, the only Sicel who tried to persuade his people to rebel against the Greeks.

The ruined city occupies a ridge overlooking a vast rolling green valley; across it you can see Mount Etna, covered in snow. The overgrown meadows that separate the theater, the agora, the altars, and the residential district are covered with white clover; the almond trees are in blossom. The site is deserted, peaceful, absolutely silent but for the sound of bells and the faint bleating of a flock of sheep grazing on a nearby hillside. It's paradise on Earth.

Some time later I read, in Alexander Stille's fascinating book, *The Future of the Past,* that Morgantina is among the most heavily ravaged of Sicily's Greek ruins, plundered by thieves and bandits in order to supply the illegal, lucrative, and thriving market in stolen antiquities, a trade with suspected ties to the Mafia and with rich and powerful clients throughout the world. And, by coincidence, after we leave Sicily for Rome, I meet, at the American Academy in Rome, an archaeologist who has spent his career digging in Sicily. When I mention our visit to Morgantina, and ask if it's true that it has suffered some of the most severe theft of any of the archaeological sites in Sicily, he says, "It would be awfully hard to say which have been most plundered. Because the fact is, if you're talking about the looting of Sicilian sites ... well, let's just say there's been a lot of competition."

In eighth-grade art class we were given rectangles of Masonite, tiles, a tile cutter, and some cement and launched into the brave new world of mosaics. Our teacher encouraged us to choose any subject we liked, provided that it was more or less figurative. I decided to make a clown. I suppose I was less concerned with originality than with being able to use all the different colors of tiles. The result was—I need hardly say—dismal; jagged bits of bathroom tile protruded from the Masonite board on which you could barely make out a big red nose, rosy cheeks, blue eyes. But our teacher said that hardly mattered. The important thing was that when we grew up and went to places like Ravenna and Venice (our future as upwardly mobile middle-class tourists was taken for granted) we would understand how difficult it had been to make those glittering ceilings and vaults, how much skill and cost and effort had been required.

It was a superfluous lesson. Mosaics speak for themselves. It's possible to assume that a great fresco might have been done by one overworked, underpaid painter, perhaps with a few assistants, but to see the cathedral of San Marco or the basilicas at Ravenna is to grasp instantly that whole teams of master craftsmen were responsible, that someone ordered and paid for all that work, for the gold that, centuries later, still catches the light and bounces it off the figures of the emperors and the saints, the patriarchs and the apostles. To decorate a church or a chapel or cathedral with mosaics is to honor and represent the divine and at the same time leave no doubt about the amount of wealth and power necessary to conceive of, and complete, an artistic project of that magnitude, that ambition.

Six hundred years after the Vandals chased the Romans into the caves once inhabited by their Bronze Age forebears and then lost control of the island to Theodoric's Ostrogoths, five hundred years after Emperor Justinian's General Belisarius annexed Sicily to the Byzantine Empire, two centuries after the Saracen conquerors built the three hundred mosques that established Palermo as the capital of Islamic civilization on Sicily and a center of art and science, the increasingly tense dissension among rival groups of Muslims—Shiites and Sunnis, Yemenis, Persians, and Berbers—made the island vulnerable to invasion by the small army of Normans, the Hells Angels of the medieval world. Former mercenaries who had hired themselves out to fight for the pope, for the Byzantines, and for local aristocrats in Normandy, the Normans had already conquered, piece by piece, much of southern Italy. By 1091, Roger I, having defeated the last pocket of Saracen resistance at Enna, declared himself Count of Sicily.

For all their toughness and ferocity, the Normans proved remarkably tolerant and capable of coexisting with—and extracting the best from—the diverse groups that preexisted their arrival. Under Roger's son and successor, Roger II, Palermo became a model of multiculturalism that combined the intellectual advances and sensual pleasures (including, it's said, the love for sweets and sherbets) of Arabic society with the vigor and crude energies of a warrior culture. And, in his aspirations to rival and surpass Byzantium, Roger II experimented with the ways in which art could advance his reputation and transform the son of a mercenary soldier into the lawful—and divinely ordained—ruler of a mighty kingdom.

What better way to demonstrate this transformation than by outdoing the Byzantines at their own game—by ordering the creation of showier and more extensive mosaics than those in the grandest Byzantine basilicas? And what better way to emphasize the connection between earthly power and divine right than to let it be known that each new building project was not merely the result of a personal whim, an expensive project requiring the levying of new taxes, but rather a sacred obligation, the fulfillment of a heavenly vow, the natural consequence of a prayer granted because God *wanted* the rule of the Norman kings to thrive and prosper? So Roger II's grandson William II made it clear that he was building Monreale with the treasure (hidden by his father) that the Virgin had shown him in a dream and that he had promised to spend on a new cathedral.

This precedent—claiming that the divine was involved in an architectural project and had even (in William's case) provided heavenly financing—was established by Roger II sometime around 1130. According to the legend that he himself seems to have generated and spread, the Norman king was on his way back from the mainland when suddenly a violent storm came up and threatened to sink his ship. But the quick-thinking Roger vowed that if God rescued him from the tempest, he would order the construction of a cathedral wherever he happened to come ashore. How convenient that God not only answered Roger's prayers, but arranged for him to land at Cefalù, just down the coast from his capital at Palermo—the perfect spot at which to locate the new bishopric that he had promised the antipope Anacletus II, whom Roger supported in his struggle against Pope Innocent II in Rome.

Work on the church was begun in 1131 and, although Roger announced that Cefalù was where he wished to be buried, it's believed that he never finished the cathedral—possibly because his rapprochement with Innocent II in 1139 diminished the urgency of his need to support his personal bishopric. Likewise, art historians have suggested that the extant mosaics represent only a fraction of a plan for something more elaborate, more on the order of what Roger would build at the Palatine Chapel in Palermo and what his grandson William would create in the cathedral at Monreale.

And yet the relative simplicity of the mosaics at Cefalù is partly what gives them their authority. At Monreale's cathedral, at the Palatine Chapel, and even at the smaller and more intimate church of La Martorana in Palermo, the multitude of scenes from the Old and New Testaments, from the lives of the saints, and from an idealized, spiritualized version of recent history (one panel at La Martorana shows Roger II accepting the crown proffered by Christ) makes it hard to focus. You simply don't know where to look first.

But at Cefalù's cathedral, there's no question. Only later do you notice the presence of the Virgin and the Apostles because your gaze tracks directly and almost involuntarily up to the image of Christ Pantocrator covering the vault above the altar. You're drawn to the face of the Pantocrator much the way iron filings are pulled toward a magnet. The face of Jesus is so commanding, so fascinating and psychologically complex, that it would probably be the thing you noticed first even if you were surrounded by the busy, cinematic distractions of the Bible stories bannered over the walls of Monreale's cathedral and the Palatine Chapel.

Anyway, there's no way to know. Because the fact is: There is nothing quite like Cefalù's Pantocrator. The Cathedral of Monreale and the Palatine Chapel are, of course, magnificent. But the difference between them and the Cathedral of Cefalù is almost like the difference between seeing some splashy Cecil B. DeMille epic when you're a child and contemplating an art masterpiece as an adult. Fittingly, the face of the Cefalù Christ includes features—a Norman pallor, an Arabic-looking beard, expressive eyebrows evocative of the Byzantine Greeks—suggestive of the diverse races that composed Roger's kingdom, and perhaps that's partly what makes the Redeemer seem so human. But it's the *quality* of his humanity—and his divinity—that finally seems so unique: The depth of understanding, the sensitivity, the grief and the ability to transcend grief, and, above all, the power of that image (made, after all, from bits of broken tile and chips of gold) to make each viewer feel that he or she is in direct, unmediated communication with those eyes, that gaze.

"I am the light of the world," says the inscription on the book that Christ is holding in his left hand while he blesses us with the right. "He who follows me he shall not walk in darkness, but shall have the light of life." And at first, it's almost possible to believe that light is shining from the image itself. But gradually, you realize how much depends on sunlight—on the light of the natural world. Especially in winter, it's best to visit the cathedral in the early morning and afternoon, when sunlight is streaming in the small window behind the mosaic. By late afternoon, it's almost too dark to see. And the effect of the light is such that the mosaics seem to be constantly changing.

After a while, the church custodian begins to recognize us, and nods when he sees us, because we keep coming back to look—every few hours, every hour, it's almost as if the image of the Pantocrator is something that's been left in our care, something we need to check on.

In accordance with his wish to be buried at Cefalù, Roger II had two marble sarcophagi installed in the Duomo. But after his death, his heirs—assisted by the ecclesiastical authorities, who no longer recognized the bishopric at Cefalù—counter-manded his desire and interred him in the massive, gloomy Cathedral of Palermo, in a plain sarcophagus, and not in the marble coffins that he had made and in which he wanted to be laid to rest. Roger's grandson Frederick II stole the marble sarcophagi back from Cefalù, in the middle of the night, right from under the knowing, sorrowful eyes of the Christ Pantocrator—and brought them to Palermo to serve as the final resting place, not for the king who had had them made, but for his father and himself.

CHAPTER SIX

Two Towns

For all my worries about not understanding enough, about being deceived by surface reality, about not seeing through to the truth of whatever I happen to be observing, still there are moments—whole days—of constant surprise, of enjoyment and happiness so pure that I'm content to exist in the moment and on the surface. I hardly care, I don't want to know, if something ugly underlies all that beauty.

On one such sunny, warm, midwinter day, we leave Cefalù and head up into the Madonie Mountains. On both sides of the road are flowering almonds, their white blossoms glowing against the background of green and yellow garden plots and fields just beginning to return to life after the brief but severe winter that can bring ice and snow to these slopes. As the road climbs, we drive through groves of olives and eucalyptus, past waterfalls and streams, old stone barns and farmhouses that—

like the baroque palazzi in Syracuse—are invitations to dream of exchanging your old life for a new one in a Sicilian hill town.

After half an hour we reach the Sanctuary of Gibilmanna, a popular pilgrimage spot that draws crowds of the faithful for the feast of the Madonna on September 8. Established by the Benedictines in the sixth century, the monastery is now home to an order of Capuchin friars, one of whom—bearded, in a rough brown cloak—is talking to some workmen doing renovations on the property. Otherwise, the place is deserted, and we wander, undisturbed, into the church and through the stone courtyards surrounded by refectories and dormitories each named after a monk or priest important in the history of the order.

Every quarter hour, the church bells toll, echoing over the valley. In a former monk's cell, a museum displays the artifacts and objects that illuminate the history and the ethos of the Capuchins, who believe in the spiritual benefits of physical labor and self-sufficiency. The perfect simplicity and function-ality of the handmade farm tools and kitchen equipment remind me of the New England Shakers, whose prayers may have differed from those of the monks, but whose daily exis-tence and essential values inspired a similar aesthetic.

The road snakes higher into the Madonies. Goats and sheep graze the olive groves and grassy hills. We keep stopping to let herds cross in front of our car; at one point we round a sharp curve to find two rams at play, bashing horns in the middle of the road. Not long after, we watch two shepherds in long, old-fashioned black woolen cloaks—like revenants from another century—ordering their dogs to control their unruly flock.

At last, we reach the hill town of Castelbuono. By now, it's late Saturday morning, almost time for lunch. When we stop and park in the piazza, the air is so full of sound that only gradually do we realize what we are hearing is the human voice, the melodic Italian of the townspeople who have gathered in the square to talk and gossip. There are no revving engines, no honking horns, no buzzing *motorini*—none of the noises that compose the street life we know.

We stop a moment, listening. People take note of our arrival, but continue their conversations, as if anything else would be an invasion of their privacy, and ours. As we look for a place to have a quick cup of coffee, the owner of the *pasticceria,* who has been chatting with friends in the square, cuts us slices of the marvelous panettone—have a taste, he says—that he has been handing out to his neighbors.

We slip into the civic museum, where the curator proudly shows us through its two rooms full of embroidered vestments once worn by local priests, wall hangings beaded with coral, and costumes bequeathed to the town by the Ventimiglia family, the influential dynasty that, in the fourteenth century, supported the Spaniards in their conflicts with the Angevins. And he tells us that we cannot leave town without seeing its eponymous castle, as well as the Chiesa Matrice Vecchia, just across the piazza.

It's an experience we'll have, with slight variations, all over the island. Especially in the smaller towns, the less frequently visited spots, you need only ask a simple question about a building, a painting, an archaeological site, a historical incident, and the person you asked will smile, light up, and launch into a long, animated explanation. People seem delighted to tell you the history of a place, a history to which they feel intimately connected. It must be one of the more positive aspects of living in a town where everyone knows you, and you know everyone, where your family has known every other family for generations. The compensations for the claustrophobic lack of privacy, freedom, and economic mobility are community and history—the pride and reassurance of feeling that you are part of a continuum, that your life is part of something larger, something that began hundreds of years before you were born and that will continue, long after you are gone.

In the church, a friendly young woman shows us the magnificent seventeenth-century polyptych depicting the Coronation of the Virgin, the frescoes of the saints decorating the pillars, holy figures made of wax set in niches in the walls. When she asks us if we want to see the crypt, we agree a little reluctantly, more out of politeness than enthusiasm, expecting what one sees under so many churches: dismal rows of sarcophagi containing the remains of the local nobility, or chilly, dripping, labyrinthine corridors lined with pillaged burial chambers.

So it comes as a surprise when she turns on the light and reveals that the walls are completely covered with brightly colored and well-preserved fifteenth-century frescoes picturing scenes from the Old and New Testaments. Deeply heartfelt and honest, the paintings plainly express the profound religious feelings of a group of local artists, and the fervor of their desire to lay spiritual claim to the underground space, to convert it from the pagan temple whose altar still exists, to make it into a Christian sanctuary.

It does seem like an enormous wealth of art treasures to find just in one small church in one small town. And, as we leave, the young woman reminds us not to miss the castle, where there is an amazing chapel decorated by Giacomo Serpotta.

In fact the castle's chapel is more amazing than we could have imagined. It's more intimate, more playful, and, in a way, more extreme—even more thickly encrusted with statuary—than the Serpotta masterpieces in Palermo: the oratories of San Lorenzo and San Domenico. A guard tells us that this is where the Ventimiglia family used to come for their prayers ... and after a moment he reminds us not to miss the town's other great church, the Matrice Nuova, the tomb of the Ventimiglias. There is, he says, another museum near the Matrice Nuova: the Museo Francesco Minà-Palumbo, a natural history museum filled with specimens assembled and botanical drawings done by a local doctor with a passion for the flora and fauna of the Madonie Mountains.

Sadly, by the time we get to the church and the museum, the town has done the vanishing act that all villages and cities do in the early afternoon, especially on Saturdays. Everything's closed. And so we promise ourselves to return, to see the treasures that remain to be seen in this art-rich mountain town, miles from anywhere, in the midst of the Madonie range.

Such mornings inevitably change the way you look at the island, the way you see a map of Sicily. Each red and black dot, each name, each stop along a winding road begins to seem like a promise, a potential trove of riches. All you have to do is stop in the piazza, park, get out of you car, and wander into the civic museum.

Yet Sicily keeps reminding you: Never assume that you know what will happen, never attempt to predict what sort of experience you will to have. There are parts of the island—the gritty suburbs of Palermo and Catania, the polluted petrochemical centers of Gela and Porto Empedocle—that make you want to close your eyes as you pass through them, though by then it's already too late, you've already inhaled enough toxic fumes and seen enough grim housing blocks.

Our literary pilgrimage to the inland town of Racalmuto to visit the birthplace of the great writer Leonardo Sciascia turns out to be the very opposite of our idyllic morning in Castelbuono. It's almost comical, really, but the problem starts when, after a brief drive up from Agrigento, we can't find a parking place. It's not an uncommon situation. Typically, the Sicilian approach to parking reflects the gap between the superficial and the essential. On the surface are the daunting blue-and-red signs with cars tipped backward and chained to tow trucks. The reality is that Sicilians leave their cars wherever they feel like it: Everybody knows your car, the cops know, the neighbors know, if someone needs to use the garage your car happens to be blocking, they know where to find you.

But Racalmuto makes you feel the way we did in Noto, the way strangers are made to feel in certain towns, mostly in the island's interior: Everyone knows everyone else—and no one knows you. No one wants to know you. And the same goes for your car.

We drive around for twenty minutes through the dusty town with nothing special to recommend it, but which nonetheless begins to seem more and more attractive as it repeatedly rejects our efforts to find a few feet of space in which to leave our vehicle. We keep glimpsing intriguing spots—a ruined castle, a handsome piazza—but there's no way to get there. And so we keep cruising the maze of one-way streets, past the same people: the men playing cards in front of the café, the women outside the vegetable stall. Perhaps it's just frustration and paranoia, but after a while it seems that they're looking at us, watching us go by, and it's not exactly friendly....

Actually, it seems like the perfectly appropriate thing to be happening in the town Sciascia wrote about so eloquently and so often, giving the place so many different names but always the same social climate and moral geography: Scratch the surface, just lightly, and what you uncover is the human equivalent of an ant colony, with its own occult laws, its limits, its prescribed patterns of behavior, and all of it ruled—ultimately, and beneath layers of subterfuge and obfuscation—by the Mafia.

A number of his novels begin in more or less the same way: A crime has been committed. Someone—a thoughtful, intelligent soul, a person of sensitivity and conscience, most often an outsider, a policeman from up north, or a sheltered linguistics professor—is assigned, or decides, to investigate. He spends most of the book tracking down the incriminating evidence that anyone who knew the town well could have supplied in the first few pages. Always, the killing is Mafia-related, and always there is some effort to dismiss it as a crime of passion arranged by some jealous husband or wife, or even some disgruntled former employee. To read Sciascia is to understand that towns like Racalmuto are closed societies, and that they have reasons, voluntary or unwilled, for remaining that way.

After a half hour that seems like an eternity, we decide we've had it. *Basta,* fine, I know what Racalmuto looks like. I've had enough. We drive out of town and feel joyous—like kids let out of school early—when we get back on the open road. Maybe it's a matter of longitude and latitude, of history, geography, or socioeconomics, but certain places do seem to have a particular character, a personality obvious even to the outsider.

In Peter Robb's excellent book, *Midnight in Sicily,* he describes his trip, by bus, to Racalmuto: Unable to find a place to eat or stay, unable to get anyone to help him or even speak to him, cold, filled with a weird dread, spooked by the sense that he was repeatedly running into the same funeral procession, he literally fled the town. Powered by the urgency of his desire to escape, he sprinted straight uphill to the nearest railroad station, where he was thrilled to find a train that would take him back to Palermo that same night.

CHAPTER SEVEN

The Wonders of the World

When I was very young my great-aunt gave me a set of the *Book of Knowledge* that had been published, I think, in the late 1920s. I used to read the encyclopedia—one volume for each letter, bound in embossed dark red with blue lettering—from cover to cover, like a novel. It was a deeply strange reading experience, since by the time I got the books a good deal of the information they contained (certainly much of the science and history) was outdated, and besides, I was too young to understand much of what I was reading. The result was that I never much knew or cared what was supposed to be factual, and what wasn't. Were the constellations really formed when Greek mythological figures were pasted up in the heavens? As far as I was concerned, they were.

One of my favorite pages was an illustration for a long article on Charles Kingsley's *Water Babies,* the Victorian children's classic. The other was a series of illustrations—I remember them as black-and-white photographs, but of course that was impossible—of the Seven Wonders of the Ancient World. The Statue of Zeus at Olympia, the Hanging Gardens of Babylon, the Colossus of Rhodes. Nothing in the text informed me (or perhaps I didn't want to know) that some of these places no longer existed, if they ever had. In any case, that was information I didn't want, since it would have interfered with my ambition to someday visit them, one by one.

Frequently, traveling in Sicily, I find myself remembering that page in the encyclopedia, because it seems to me that what I am seeing, that what I am lucky enough to be seeing, is as close as I will ever come to the Seven Wonders of the Ancient World. Perhaps it has something to do with the fact that so many astonishing places are so close together. Within a single day you could, if you wished—given enough stamina and a really hot car—visit Segesta, probably the most majestically sited Greek temple and theater in Sicily; then you could head west to Mozia, the ghostly island that was once the home of an important Phoenician settlement; and, finally, drive north, slightly east, and then straight up to Erice, a town so exquisite that it became the raw material for legends and was, for centuries, the center of the cult of the goddess Aphrodite. You *could* see all three places in one day, but each of them makes you want to stay (only in Erice is it possible to spend the night) or to keep returning to watch the effects of the changing weather and the mercurial Sicilian light.

What Segesta, Mozia, and Erice share in common is that they are not only lovely, but mysterious. No one knows why the

temple at Segesta was left unfinished (there is no roof, and the thick columns were never fluted) or exactly when it was built, though most scholars agree that it was constructed in the fifth century B.C., by the citizens of Egesta, a settlement of Hellenized Elymians, members of one of the earliest indigenous groups—the same tribe that founded Eryx, as Erice was originally known.

In their ongoing battle with their rivals in Selinunte, the Egestans repeatedly switched sides, allying themselves with the various factions and city-states warring for control of the island. In one famous story, the Egestans—hoping to convince the Athenian envoys that they would be wealthy and useful allies—rounded up all the gold and silver vessels from neighboring towns (including Eryx) and moved them around to each of the houses that the Athenians visited.

Lonely, moody, surrounded by mountains, overlooking the patchwork fields in the valley below and (from the theater, a brief bus ride uphill from the temple) a vista that extends all the way to the Gulf of Castellammare, Segesta is one of those places where the sky itself seems to expand (as it does, say, above the Grand Canyon) as if in response to the heroic scale of what lies beneath it. For centuries it has been the sort of popular tourist destination that has inspired romantic voyagers and travel writers to contemplate the sublimity and transience of earthly existence, the vast scope of eternity. And, indeed, Segesta makes you see why their musings might have led them in those reverent, transcendent, and gloomy directions.

When Goethe visited Segesta the site had not yet been restored and, tired from the effort of "clambering about among the unimpressive ruins of a theater," he cut his visit short. And yet his description of the temple's setting still seems fresh, accurate and recognizable: "The site of the temple is remarkable. Standing on an isolated hill at the head of a long, wide valley and surrounded by cliffs, it towers over a vast landscape ... The countryside broods in a melancholy fertility; it is cultivated but with scarcely a sign of human habitation ... The wind howled around the columns as though they were a forest, and birds of prey wheeled, screaming, above the empty shell."

When we arrive in Erice after the brief but dramatic drive from Trapani—a series of hairpin turns providing vertiginously seductive vistas of the sea and the cliffs below and taking us up almost 2,500 feet in less than half an hour—the town seems as

deserted, as lonely as Segesta. It's midafternoon, on an unusually bright (Erice is famous for the mists and fog in which it is
often shrouded) and chilly Saturday in February. Too narrow for
cars, the cobblestone alleys of the medieval town are so quiet
that we can hear our footsteps. Strangely, it reminds me of
walking, late at night, along the quietest canals and through
the emptiest, most wintry piazzas of Venice. The sense of solitude is so eerie that my heart speeds up when we turn a corner
and see other people: a couple of expensively dressed Italian
tourists ascending the steep street. What are they doing here—
and why is she carrying that Fendi shopping bag?

It's the perfect time to visit Erice. You want to be here
when no one else is, very early in the morning, in the quiet of
an off-season afternoon, or late at night. For to be in Erice is to
indulge your fantasies of time travel, of what it would be like
to live in the fourteenth century, to see its ghosts come alive, to
lose all contact with modern life. Gazing out from the parapets
of the fortress and the twelfth-century castle, looking down
across the sea (supposedly on especially clear days you can see
all the way to Africa) you feel as if you've left the world behind,
down below, and that the only way to rejoin it is to let go and
plummet straight down. For many reasons, Erice is not the first
place I'd recommend to the acrophobic.

It's hard to imagine what this place would be like on a
summer day, when the narrow streets and tiny piazzas are
choked with pedestrian traffic. I'd been oddly resistant to
coming here, partly for fear of finding a crowded souvenir
bazaar. Yesterday, at our hotel in Trapani, I heard an American
businessman say he was planning to "buzz" up to Erice—he

pronounced it "Aero-shade," so that at first I thought he meant some trendy Italian design firm—to buy some "trinkets" before his flight home the next day. I'd also feared that it might turn out to be just another pretty hill town, like dozens of other towns we'd visited in Italy and France. I've always loved those towns—but now I worry that the attractions of Erice might seem a little thin after the glory and monumentality of Segesta.

But Erice, as it turns out, is not just another hill town. The height, the view, the sweep of ocean and hills below—it seems almost laughable that any place could be so lovely. But the town itself is sobering, so austere that it makes cities like Gubbio or the most melancholy Provençal mountain village seem as cozy as a New England hamlet, as sensual as a Polynesian island. Erice is so severe and frosty that being here feels like how it must feel to be inside a diamond; its perfection is almost physically painful, as if its edges were as sharp—and as cutting—as a diamond's.

Even the paving stones are aesthetically satisfying. The grass that grows up through the crevices between the polished stones arranged in regular geometric patterns is such a pleasing shade of green it could have been chosen from a catalog. It looks more like set design than like an organic, living town. Except for the televisions tuned to the sports-and-racing channels in the few cafés that are open, except for an occasional car braving the capillary-thin streets to deliver luggage to one of the town's hotels, there is nothing to spoil the illusion that we have left our own century and moved back into another.

Erice's beauty—and the fact that we know so little about the town's history and origins—has created a sort of vacuum into which people have, for thousands of years, been moved to throw myths and legends, like propitiatory offerings. Something so perfect—and so undocumented, so unaccounted for—must surely have its roots in divinity. And so we hear that the Temple of Aphrodite-Venus was founded by Aeneas, who landed here to perform the funeral rites for his father, whom he had rescued on his shoulders from the sack of Troy; because a fire had destroyed some of Aeneas's ships, he was obliged to leave behind several of his men, who became the town's first residents. Daedalus is said to have worked on the Temple of Aphrodite; it was here that he designed, as a gift for the goddess, a honeycomb made entirely of gold. And, according to legend, the goddess herself came here to live with her lover, the Argonaut Butes, whom she rescued from the sea after the Sirens' song enticed him to jump into the ocean. Heracles, too, is supposed to have stopped by on his way home from carrying off the cattle of Geryon—and, during his stay, killed the Elymian king who tried to steal them.

Yet these stories seem too vital, too full of life and health and ingenuity and sex to have much to do with Erice. Because the strange thing is that what's most beautiful about the place is how dead it is, how unchanged and unchanging, how perfectly preserved, like an exquisite corpse embalmed by some alchemical formula of altitude, wind, fog, and water.

Suddenly, I know what Erice reminds me of: Les Baux-de-Provence, the ruined medieval town that sits on a hilltop in the south of France, rising out of the living town beneath it. There's that same sense of seeing something that will never change, or change much, that will remain untouched by the forces that keep shaping and refashioning whatever is alive—that is, by life itself. To walk the streets of Erice and then drive back down to Trapani is almost like being Persephone—like being permitted to enter the realm of the dead and then return to the noisy, disorderly, and precious province of the living.

From the start, the prospect of going to Mozia makes me a little edgy—the idea of sailing across a lagoon to an island on which no one lives, an island that was once the outpost of a highly developed and cruel civilization, but where there are now only its ruins and a small museum in the former home of Joseph Whitaker, one of the Englishmen who came to Sicily and sensibly intuited that a fortune could be made by exporting Marsala wine.

In winter, the museum (and, by extension, the island) closes at one in the afternoon. I can't help thinking that, unlikely as it seems ... what if the fisherman who ferries us out there gets distracted and forgets about us, and we're stuck out there all night? What if we're stranded, exposed to the elements, alone with the spirits of the Phoenician traders who first came to Mozia in the eighth century B.C. and who lived in harmony with their Greek neighbors until the Carthaginian wars, when Dionysius the Elder of Syracuse, using catapults, missiles, and battering rams—state-of-the-art tools of fourth-century warfare—destroyed the settlement and much of its population?

I phone ahead from Trapani and the woman who answers at the museum gives me directions for finding the ferry port, roughly halfway between Trapani and Marsala. The signs

Boatman, Mozia

directing us to Mozia and the port—just a parking lot, really, beside a small building, with a solitary fishing boat waiting at the dock—are reassuring. It's not exactly unexplored wilderness, uncharted territory. Going to Mozia—and back—is something people do. All the time.

But not, as it happens, today. The fisherman working on his nets at the back of his boat seems delighted that the morning has brought him at least a little business. He couldn't be friendlier as he points out the postcard-pretty view from his boat of the windmills and the salt pans for which the western coast of Sicily is famous; he shows me where to sit for shelter from the brisk wind. The ride isn't long—about ten, maybe fifteen minutes. The water is so shallow and still that we could probably swim if we had to. And the boatman is very clear about the fact that he'll be back to pick us up in two hours. Still, as he lets us off at the dock that serves as the island's small harbor, I feel a sharp, irrational stab of panic and abandonment.

Fortunately, my anxiety dissipates as we head toward the museum up the walkway, lined on both sides with plants sending up shoots topped with giant scarlet flowers. Stopping in the tidy villa-museum to orient ourselves, and to reassure ourselves that there is indeed another living human on the island, I find myself grinning with loony gratitude at the young man who takes our money and gives us tickets.

He suggests that we tour the museum before we explore the island, and as we walk into the first of the few small rooms that compose the Museo Whitaker, we stop short in front of the "Ephebus of Mozia," the fifth-century B.C. statue so arresting and shockingly beautiful that it occurs to me that, two hours from now, the ferry could return and find us still standing here, staring at the sculpture.

The marble statue of the young man, the ephebus, was discovered in the northern part of the island, near the temple area. It had been buried, lying on its back, covered with stones— hidden, it is thought, during the ghastly siege of Dionysius, in the hopes that someone would remember to dig it up after the war was over. But no one was left, or anyway no one who knew or remembered, and the "Young Man of Mozia" remained in his untimely grave until the late nineteenth century, when he was exhumed, first his torso, and then, years later, his head.

For weeks, we have been looking at Greek statuary. In fact it's often seemed as if Sicily has as many archaeological museums as it has orange groves, that every small town has its own brown (denoting a cultural attraction) sign featuring the logo of a temple and an arrow pointing to the local repository of coins and pottery sherds. What's surprising is how many of these modest, unpromising museums contain a minor masterpiece. Less surprisingly, the larger and richer institutions are fascinating. To browse among their collections of vases figured with masked actors, flute players, dancing girls, centaurs and satyrs, maenads and Amazons is the closest we can hope to come to watching an animated film of the daily existence and imaginative lives of the Greek colonists in Sicily. Always, there are funerary artifacts—a basket of figs carved from stone to insure that the dead would eat well in their afterlife—and sculptures of young men with exquisitely rendered musculature and shapely bodies

In Syracuse's Museo Archeologico Regionale Paolo Orsi is a magnificent headless kouros—a statue of a nude young man; in the archaeological museum at Agrigento is the celebrated "Ephebus of Agrigento," the figure of a young male athlete believed to have been a star of the Olympic Games. But compared to the "Young Man of Mozia," those other pieces now seem lifeless, abstract, devoid of personality and spirit. Indeed, it's hard to believe that the "Young Man of Mozia" and the "Ephebus of Agrigento" could have been sculpted in the same century.

There is nothing anywhere like the "Young Man of Mozia." For not until Michelangelo would a sculptor again prove able to breathe so much life into marble, to make stone so exactly mimic flesh, and to celebrate the sensuality of the young male body with such control and such impassioned admiration. The "Ephebus of Mozia" is at once fully male and completely androgynous, like some representative of an earlier, mythic race—before humans were divided into males and females. Clothed in a tight-fitting tunic that closely follows the lines of his thighs and buttocks, his head turned to one side, his features caught in an expression partway between strength and submission, his hand resting lightly on his outthrust hip, the "Young Man" is so frankly sensual, the effect of the work is so unmistakably erotic that I'm glad there's no one else in the museum, no other tourists on the island. It would be ... embarrassing to look at the statue with strangers around; it's something you want to do in private.

At last, we manage to free ourselves from the statue's spell and head out across the island, along the sandy pathways lined with scrub pines and dwarf palms, the dirt tracks through the vineyards, the fields of poppies and wildflowers that cover much of the flat, open land. We pass the remains of a black-and-white mosaic floor, the so-called domestic quarters, the sacred and "industrial areas" where the Phoenicians tanned leather, dyed textiles, and baked pottery. And finally we reach the necropolis, a collection of tombs—the horrifyingly miniature sarcophagi that were used to bury the children killed in the Phoenician religious rituals and later (when the custom of infant sacrifice was no longer practiced) the small animals that were substituted as sacrificial victims.

Seagulls shriek overhead and dive toward the white beach. We can hear and smell and see the steely ocean. The grape arbors and wildflowers surround us. The prettiness of the scenery contrasts so sharply with the loneliness, the melancholy, and the sheer creepiness of the necropolis that I begin to shiver in the warm morning sun. And, once more, I find myself praying that the boatman will remember we're out here.

Mozia

Which, of course, he does. At precisely the appointed time, we watch his neat white boat putter up the dock. On the way back to the mainland—a trip that, naturally, seems even shorter than the voyage out—he stops to pick up a friend from another boat, who's been fixing his nets and baiting traps. Then our boatman turns to me and asks where we're from. When I tell him we live in New York, he asks (as so many Sicilians do) about the twin towers and (like so many Sicilians) expresses his sympathy and his conviction that life must go on. He tells me that his son lives in the United States, he's opened five restaurants in Boston and is about to start one in Miami. After a while, I think to ask him what kind of wine is made from the grapes on the island.

Marsala, he says. Always. They still make Marsala.

The next day, in Sciacca, we go into a fancy wine store to buy a bottle of Marsala. We ask the proprietor what's the best, the driest … and he tells us: This is dry, this is good, the best. But maybe he misunderstood us, or maybe we got something wrong, because in fact it's not very good. It's too sweet, cloying, with a harsh after-bite. We think: This can't be right. It can't be the wine from Mozia. We'd expected something more, something special and sublime—something finer to have grown up from the bones and dust of the dead Phoenicians.

CHAPTER EIGHT

The Conversation

Probably, to be honest, the main reason why I want to be reborn as an Italian in general and a Sicilian man in particular has to do with my envy of a certain kind of conversation. The exchange takes place in a restaurant, it unfolds in its own time, it has an unhurried ritualistic quality, it transpires between the waiter or the restaurant owner and the customer, it begins with the words *che consiglia,* what do you suggest, or, more coloquially, *consigliamo,* advise us. Then the conversation starts, the slow, pleasurable recital of the possibilities, the choices to be selected from the day's menu, the antipasti, the *primi* and *secondi,* the *contorni,* the consideration and discussion, the back and forth: What's best, what's freshest, what's just come in from the market, the sea, the farm, the woods, how it is prepared, the ingredients, the seasonings—it's almost as if the meal is being eaten before it is even ordered.

In theory, I could have that conversation. I know enough Italian and, as it happens, my vocabulary is particularly strong on words having to do with food, the kitchen, the menu. There is probable nothing, or very little, I couldn't understand, none of those slow pleasurable decisions I wouldn't feel qualified to make. And yet I never have it. I look at the menu, I decide, I order, the food comes. We eat.

In fact, I've had something approaching the conversation a few times during our stay in Sicily. In a trattoria in Syracuse, I asked the waiter about the specialties of the house, and what he replied seemed so improbable—fusilli with tiny shrimp and fresh pumpkin—that I ordered it partly to see if he'd said what I thought he'd said. He *had,* and the dish *was* improbable—and delicious. In an *osteria,* also in Syracuse, but one which specializes in the inland cooking of Ragusa, the owner recited the list of what was available (there was no printed menu), then went through it again and again. Each time the list grew shorter, and I knew he was editing as he went along, making the selections for us, based on something he was gathering from our responses, or perhaps he was just telling us what he liked best: an antipasti plate composed of slices of different sorts of *tortas*—little pies baked with ricotta and vegetables—followed by a risotto with squash blossoms and cream, and tagliatelle with homemade sausage and ricotta.

In a restaurant in Cefalù—perhaps my favorite of all the places at which we ate in Sicily—the problem was solved for me. An extra page had been added to the menu, a list of specials entitled, *"Il chef consiglia."* The chef advises! Without my even having to ask, and with everything printed out, so I could read it at my leisure, with time to understand, and even to look up the few words I didn't recognize. And what delights the chef advised in this seaside paradise that had managed to broker a happy marriage of innovation and tradition, to retain the *sapori di Sicilia,* the flavors of Sicily, the particularly Sicilian mix of sweet and sour and salty, to serve them in the large, traditional-sized portions (no stingy nouvelle cuisine presentation-is-everything theater here) and at the same time refine and readjust the recipes according to the most up-to-the-minute notions of *la cucina stagionale,* seasonal cooking.

Many of the dishes contained in their titles the word *invernali,* winter, which in this case (it was mid-February) meant artichokes, prepared in every imaginable fashion. The antipasti plate included freshly cooked and marinated artichoke hearts, arranged among leaves of wild greens and radicchio and huge shrimp, *gamberoni,* boiled red. Shrimp and artichokes reappeared atop the homemade tagliatelle, black with cuttlefish ink, and in ravioli—the pasta stuffed with artichokes and sauced with shrimp and fresh tomatoes. But the standout, the menu's most inspired creation, was a new take on *involtini di pesce spada,* rolled swordfish, a Sicilian standard, cooked, in this case, *all' arancia,* with wedges of orange and an orange sauce, stuffed with breadcrumbs and parsley, and seasoned with capers, raisins, anchovies, pine nuts, and orange zest.

In the absence of such cross-cultural culinary thoughtfulness (il chef consiglia!), another approach to ordering without the preliminary conversation is to linger over the bread and wine long enough to see what other people are eating—and then just point. This works particularly well in a neighborhood restaurant, during a leisurely weekend lunch.

On a Sunday afternoon, in Syracuse, we watched large families ordering one dish at a time: first a plate of fried shrimp, then bowls of fat mussels steamed with garlic and parsley, then a portion of grilled calamari. We did more or less as they did, all the time longing for a big Sicilian family of our own, or at least enough people to expand the range and scope of what we could sensibly order. What makes this method possible is that, in Sicily as in most of Italy, no one cares much if you order everything at once, or in stages; if the swordfish in the pasta with eggplant and pesce spada is particularly good, go ahead and order swordfish for your second course, sliced thin and grilled, or lightly breaded and fried, *alla palermitana.*

Still, the learn-by-watching-your-neighbors approach requires a certain amount of attention and vigilance, however relaxed. It took a few tries to figure out that the plates of shellfish were not appearing automatically, by magic, on the tables of the patrons at the restaurants in the little harbor of Capo di Molino. As they'd walked in, they'd made their choices from the displays of seafood on ice outside on the sidewalk: oysters, shrimp, and fresh sea urchins waiting to be sliced open and scooped out. We watched and learned, and did the same.

But it's not precisely the same as having that long, sustained consideration, that relaxed introduction to the joys of the meal before us. Partly, our problem is simply that we aren't from the neighborhood; many of the waiters and customers know each other, they're friends, they went to school together, they exchange warm handshakes, local gossip, or even hugs as they walk into the restaurant and ask after the health of one another's families. This is especially true of those solitary men—a widower who lives nearby, or someone who works in the neighborhood—who come in alone. The prelunch conversation lasts longer than it takes to eat the meal, which is slapped down, consumed at breakneck speed, and the diner leaves as quickly as he arrived.

Another thing that keeps us from having that preprandial conversation is, obviously, cultural. Americans aren't used to it; at home, we just don't do it. At good restaurants, waiters recite the list of specials and then, more often than not, take a deep breath of relief at having successfully got through their personal mini-ordeal. The especially daring or altruistic waiter may suggest that this or that dish is particularly good tonight, but in general that's the end of it—not the beginning, as it would be in Sicily.

And who can blame American waiters for their hesitation? Americans make fun of servers who are perceived to be excessively outgoing or chatty. Their personalities are considered too big for their jobs, their friendliness inappropriate, intrusive, an invasion of the diners' privacy, an abrogation of our God-given individual American freedom to choose for ourselves. It's almost as if the waiter had followed us into the election booth and was telling us how to vote. And though I have heard the waiters in my neighborhood coffee shop in New York say that that day's chicken noodle or pea soup is particularly good, it rarely happens that your counter person at the roadside diner or local lunch joint will be asked about, or spontaneously begin to praise, the virtues of the grilled cheese or the hamburger deluxe.

And so it's only natural, or in any case, cultural, that something of that reticence and anxiety should persist among

Americans abroad. We think of ourselves as decisive people, we're wary of uncertainty, of seeming not to know what we want, of taking up a waiter's time, of seeking and taking advice. Suppose he suggests some delicacy we can't afford, or some ingredient we don't like, or are allergic to? (One thing that does seem to make this easier for the Sicilians is the fact that their food tastes are, in general, so much broader, so much less picky than ours, and also that their menus list so little that hasn't been familiar to them since childhood.) We Americans can't help but worry: Will the waiter be insulted if we ignore his suggestions and shake our heads and return to our strained perusals of the menu? Will the whole conversation turn out to have been a mistake, a source of misunderstanding and embarrassment that will linger throughout the meal?

In any case, I gradually come to realize that my difficulty in having the conversation is not entirely a matter of culture but also of gender. For in Sicily the waiters are nearly always male, and though you do see women working in the kitchen and managing restaurants, it's mostly in places run by entire families. Female chefs certainly exist, but—just as in the United States—they're much more rare than their male counterparts. And while women may be dining alone in restaurants in Milan, or ordering the wine for their entire party in Rome, or chatting up the waiters in Venice, the fact is I've rarely seen this even in northern Italian cities (except when the customer is a female foreign tourist) and almost never in Sicily.

Anyone who doubts that Sicily is still a patriarchal society should note how rarely women are entrusted with the job of preparing and serving food, or encouraged to work outside the home in such an intimate relation with strangers. Because the fact is, it is intimate: Two men talking about the food about to be served resemble, in more than casual ways, two men talking about women, or sex. There's that same sense of appreciation, of remembered or anticipated enjoyment, that shared knowledge of pleasure.

Which all contributes to the reason why I find the conversation so difficult. As flawed as my Italian is, I'm more comfortable speaking it than Howie is. And though any waiter can quickly figure out why I'm the one doing the talking, it still seems to unnerve him to be having the conversation with me when there's a perfectly intelligent man sitting right there at the table. Will my husband be affronted, will his honor be insulted as he witnesses this intense, focused exchange between his wife and another man? No doubt there *were* men, in the Sicily of just a few generations ago, who were killed for less.

One consequence is that I'm always extremely happy on those rare occasions when I find myself being cooked for, and brought food by, women—with whom, in theory, it might be possible for me to have the conversation. And so perhaps the most gratifying and enjoyable—if not exactly the most exquisite or refined—meal of our stay takes place in Scopello, a tiny fishing village on the northern coast, an hour or so from Trapani.

With its bleached craggy boulders and palm trees, its deserted white beaches bordering an ocean striated into bands of green and blue, Scopello looks, in photographs, almost like a Caribbean resort. But the day we arrive is freezing. A light drizzle had begun to mist the windshield on our drive from Palermo. And by the time we pull into town—a single cobbled street lined with

Howard Michels and Francine Prose, Scopello

quaint shops and fishermen's houses, all closed for the season, shuttered to keep out the winter cold—a driving rain is lashing the village, and the wind is blowing so fiercely that our umbrellas keep folding up and turning in on themselves.

Fortunately, I've called ahead, to a place called Torre Bennistra, where a sweet-voiced woman has informed me that she has no bread, she's closed, but … how many people are we? Two? All right, come on. *Va bene.*

When I ask directions at the local bar, a woman tells us that Torre Bennistra is definitely closed for the season. But we persevere and find it, and knock on the door of the obviously deserted restaurant. Through the window, we watch a small, stocky, old woman with curly hair and glasses, wearing an apron, get up from her chair in front of the fireplace where she has been sitting, weaving a basket. She opens the door. Ah yes, we're the ones who called, she's apologizing for something, we're apologizing, the wind is blowing so loudly we can hardly hear, yes, she'll cook us lunch but it will be very simple. *Naturale.* Fine, we say, simple is good, naturale is fine.

She waves at the empty restaurant and laughs. Have a seat, it's our choice, we can take any table we want. When Howie goes off to the bathroom, the Signora sits down at the table with me, takes out a pencil and a pad of paper. The conversation is about to begin.

She asks if Howie is my husband, if we have children, if my parents are Sicilian. She says that the weather is awful, *una giornata brutta,* a nasty day, just yesterday it was beautiful. Then she asks what we want to eat. Antipasti? Yes, I say, and she writes down, two antipasti. Pasta? Yes, I say. It's the ideal conversation, because there are no choices, she knows what we want, she knows what she can make—it's what she might make for family lunch if we weren't there. It's what she has in the house. The only choice is between more and less. So fine, let's have more. Meat or fish? Fish. Fried fish? That will be fine. Tomato salad? She writes it all down and disappears into the kitchen.

By the time we've finished our antipasti—olives and marinated raw tuna preserved by the Signora herself, a slice of salami, fresh bread—a French couple has come in, and the Signora brings out four plates of steaming pasta with a sauce that's a local specialty, *alla trapanese,* made with chopped uncooked tomatoes, basil, parsley, good olive oil, and more minced raw garlic than you could dream of serving, at home, to your most intimate friends. But of course it's marvelous, as is the fish, a whole fish for each of us, cut into three large sections, lightly breaded and fried, head, bones, tail, and all. Part of what makes this simple meal taste so especially good is that it has been prepared with such affection, and for us alone (or almost alone). It is the fulfillment of a certain sort of travel fantasy: the Sicilian mama who cooks for you, just as she would cook for her own children.

We thank the Signora profusely, we tell her it was the perfect meal for una giornata brutta, we take her picture, she insists we go out on the rainswept terrace to look at the stormy ocean, she swears that it's usually beautiful, *bello,* she points to the poster on the wall that makes Scopello look like a beach in the Bahamas. We assure her that it doesn't matter, that's how good the food was. She wipes her hands on her apron.

"*Tutto semplice,*" she says. "*Tutto naturale.*"

But of course it's naturale, semplice. That's the secret of Sicilian food, it's all in the ingredients, the very best, the very freshest elements prepared with the minimum of needless complication, pretension, or fuss, and with the maximum personal style. The Sicilian culinary palette, the vocabulary of its kitchen is—as any Sicilian cook will tell you—a relatively limited one. Olive oil, garlic, flour, eggs, ricotta, fish on the coast, meat inland. But every cook prepares every one of those same dishes just a little differently so that no two tomato sauces are the same, one cook's *pasta con sarde* (that sublime, uniquely Sicilian concoction of sardines, pine nuts, raisins, fennel, and bread crumbs) will never be mistaken for another's. It's thought that the sweet, salty, and sour flavors in pasta con sarde are (like the regional passion for ice cream and sweets) a legacy of the

Saracens. Indeed, much of Sicilian cuisine is the fortunate result of centuries of foreign invasion.

In her cookbook, *La Cucina Siciliana di Gangivecchio,* Wanda Tornabene remarks that the "painful defeats" suffered by her country are responsible for the variety of its cuisine. "Each culture—from the Greeks, Romans and Arabs to the French and Spanish—has left behind its own imprint on our eating habits." The Greeks brought their grapes, olives, and honey, the Romans their wheat and grains, the Saracens their "love of all things sweet, from sweet-and-sour dishes to sauces and candies." Moreover, the characteristic dishes of each part of the island have been heavily influenced by the culture that dominated that region; thus the Arabs bequeathed couscous to the citizens of Trapani and western Sicily.

To understand why Sicilian food is so good, just visit the markets. Whenever we arrive in a new place, the market is frequently our first destination, because each market is unique and tells you something about the character of the city. Located in the semicircular arcade of the Piazza Mercato del Pesce, with the ocean just behind it, Trapani's market is small, sweet, and low-key, though it's the only one in which the vendors call out to us and expend some energy on trying to sell us something. Perhaps it's because the city gets so few tourists in midwinter—perhaps they imagine we've moved into town and might actually be able to do something with a half kilo of monkfish liver or a chunk of pressed *bottarga,* tuna roe.

It's partly because of architecture that the fish market in Catania seems so raw and primal that it's almost scary; it's the kind of place that you hope your vegetarian friends—the ones who still eat fish—never get around to visiting. A sort of balcony or balustrade runs along one side of the market, from which you can look down on the action below—which, from that angle, suggests a killing floor or the site of some ancient, bloody sacrificial ritual being enacted by members of a secret cult or guild. The faces of the vendors are reddened by the wind, their hands scarred and thickened. The smell is powerful, to say the least, and the light takes on a silvery-blue cast as it shines on, and is reflected by, the scales of the fish; the silver-blue is intensified by contrast with the red blood and the red tarpaulins stretched over the stalls.

At the same time, everything seems clean and orderly, aesthetically arranged, the garfish and the eels in silvery rings, the small pink rouget in tidy rows with their heads up, like the glittering tiles of a mosaic. It's as if each vendor is trying to outdo the others with the beauty of his presentation, the perfect color coordination of each display. And it's remarkably educational. From watching the fish sellers in Catania, we learn how to bone sardines (by hand, pulling the skeleton out with your thumbs) and how to open sea urchins (cut the top off with scissors and, with one flick of the wrist, shake out the dirt and sand, leaving the sweet center inside). And so the market begins to seem less like a sacrificial blood feast than like an anatomical dissecting theater, a temple of science and study.

We eat lunch at the small trattoria right in the market. From our table, over plates of *pasta ai ricci* and grilled swordfish, we watch a fishmonger slice into a tuna that must weigh eighty pounds, a creature so impressive and awe-inspiring that the other vendors gather around with their hands behind their

Market, Catania

backs and just stand there staring reverently at the tuna. Eventually, without leaving our table we watch the whole thing break down, as the lunch hour begins, and each stall shuts up, the men go home—and the market disappears completely, as if it had all been a mirage.

The markets of Palermo are—like its people—the most varied and the most fascinating in their variety. Though some southwestern cities—Mazara del Vallo, for example—host sizable numbers of Tunisian fishermen and guest workers, only the capital has a population of recent immigrants from Africa, Asia, and the Middle East substantial enough to create a visibly diverse community, notably different from the rest of Sicily, where generations of assimilation have mostly homogenized the identifiable differences between the groups who have inhabited the island, though from time to time you will see a

Market, Palermo

particularly Arabic face or, alternatively, one with the fair hair and blue eyes of the Normans.

Most travelers head for the Vucciria, the oldest of Palermo's markets, so it's common to see busloads of tourists gingerly picking their way over the stones slimed with vegetable peels and slicks of offal. But my favorite market is the Ballaro; it's larger, at once friendlier and more serious, and certainly more theatrical. Advertising their wares, calling out to prospective customers, the vendors sound like exotic birds in a tropical jungle. It's a real cornucopia: mounds of artichokes with their leaves and stems still attached, piled three feet high; truckloads of *broccoletti* the size of basketballs that, with their odd purple and lime green coloring, look more like space aliens than culti- vated vegetables. Each lemon and almond has its proper place, every olive stall—decorated with stalks of rosemary—is unlike any other; the conical heaps of spices, herbs, and dried legumes resemble something you'd find in an Asian bazaar. There's so much bounty on display and for sale that even though you know that the Ballaro is located in the center of one of Palermo's poorest neighborhoods, you can almost—at least for the time it takes to walk through the market—believe there is enough food in the world.

What the markets remind you of, and partly explain, is the earthiness at the heart of Sicilian cuisine. Nothing has been sanitized, there's nothing squeamish or repressed about the Sicilian appetite, the Sicilian diet. In the *sfogliatelle*—the pastry coated with confectioners' sugar and stuffed with fresh ricotta—we're served for breakfast in Enna, the lightly sweetened filling still retains the tang of sheep's milk. Fried fish arrives on your plate, bones, head, tail, and all. One of the most exquisite Sicilian dishes consists of tiny fish served, barely cooked, over pasta or else raw with lemon; it's called *neonata*—which, of course, means newborn. You can't help thinking that if anything on the American table is newborn or even underage, we don't want to know about it, just as we make ample use of plastic wrap and packaging to spare ourselves the knowledge that what we are eating was ever alive.

In Sicily, by contrast, diners want to be assured—and rightly so—that what they are eating was *recently* alive. Whole lambs and goats and rabbits hang in the market place, not far from the stalls where you can buy and consume a plate of freshly opened sea urchins, or a chickpea or potato fritter, or a spleen sandwich, and savor it not far from a dog who happens to be enjoying a piece of raw chicken. There's nothing forced or self-conscious about Sicilian cuisine; no one talks about comfort food because it *is* comfort food. There's no nostalgia involved, because *la cucina siciliana* was never lost and rediscovered, never saved from the vile encroachments of the fast-food industry.

Nightly, on TV, you can watch advertisements for various disgusting products, including a sort of frozen patty made from a yellowish mozzarella and neon-pink prosciutto, covered with bread crumbs, equally suitable for the frying pan or the toaster oven. And the supermarket freezer sections offer such laborsaving items as zucchini flowers, breaded and prefried, needing only a brief immersion in hot oil or perhaps a few seconds in the microwave. But the energy and the vitality of the markets prove how much Sicilians are still cooking, as we say, from scratch. Anyone who wants to observe the reverence with which la cucina is still approached might want to drop by Palermo's church of La Martorana early on a weekday morning, when the parishioners leave their grocery bags by the altar so that what they are taking home from the market can be blessed by the parish priest.

What arrives at your table in Sicily represents the culmination of a tradition. At Gangivecchio, the fourteenth-century Benedictine abbey that the Tornabene family has converted into an inn known all over the island and—thanks to the cookbooks authored by Wanda Tornabene and her daughter Giovanna—the wider world, that tradition functions like a special ingredient seasoning the meals that its lucky guests are served.

Part of Gangivecchio's charm derives from the contrast between the patrician, aristocratic setting—the pergola covered with greenery, the fountain decorated with lions' heads, the cobbled walkways, the courtyard of the abbey—and the rustic simplicity of the meals offered in its dining rooms: homemade pasta with a thick mushroom *ragù,* bean soup, crêpes stuffed with ricotta and covered with a delicate spinach sauce, homemade sausage, fried sweet and savory dumplings, and huge pork shanks that can't help but increase the affection you feel for the gargantuan, bristled pig slumbering placidly in its pen near the inn.

The history of Gangivecchio is an archetypically Sicilian one: a story in which trouble and peril is, through determination, common sense, hard work, stubbornness, and a certain canniness, transformed into an occasion for triumph against all probable odds. The Tornabenes trace the history of their home back to a twelfth-century B.C. village, Engio, which antedated the Greeks, and which stood on the house's current site. Successively decimated and revived (the town was forcibly evacuated after the revolt of the Sicilian Vespers in 1282), the town of Gangi recovered and the abbey thrived until 1653, when the population of the monastery was reduced to a single monk, left to guard the property and collect taxes. Rebuilt by a local squire in the eighteenth century, the estate passed from the church's hands into private ownership, and in 1856 came into the possession of the Tornabene family.

The family cultivated the land, planting the orchards of cherries, apples, figs, pears, and nuts, tending the herb and vegetable gardens, raising cows and chickens for eggs and cheese. But in the late 1970s, the declining agricultural economy and steeply rising taxes made Gangivecchio's future seem precarious until Wanda Tornabene (with the encouragement of a local priest) decided to turn her skill in the kitchen into a business and opened a small restaurant. Gradually, the restaurant was expanded into the simultaneously luxe and rustic *agroturismo* inn at which (in rooms converted from the former monks' cells) it is possible to spend the night after you have eaten and drunk too much to even consider getting back on the road.

Surrounded by unspoiled countryside, Gangivecchio is about ten minutes by a winding lane from the town of Gangi, which is itself an hour and a half, or two hours—depending on the nationality and age of the driver—by mountain roads and then autostrada to Palermo. Over meals, you can observe the Italian guests—mostly prosperous Palermitans—in varying stages of annoyance at the fact that their cell phones will only work (and not especially well) from the dining room at the inn.

Wanda and Giovanna have written two cookbooks, one of which, *La Cucina Siciliana di Gangivecchio,* was published in 1996 and won that year's James Beard Foundation Award for Excellence. In the process they have transformed their home into the sort of earthly paradise which fuels Americans' (and, for all I know, other Sicilians') dreams of living amid the glories of Renaissance ecclesiastical architecture and Italian bucolic splendor. When we arrive and when we leave, other Americans are wandering dreamily through the gardens, as are groups of Italians, large parties who arrive for Sunday lunch and young couples who come for Saturday dinner and to stay the night. Judging from the mood of these young lovers—oddly jangled and tense, given the serenity of the surroundings—you can't help thinking that Gangivecchio may have become a destination to which upper-middle-class kids head on the first date serious enough to involve sex, or the one on which marriage will be discussed or even proposed.

And yet, as Sicily keeps reminding you, no paradise is without its price. On Saturday night, Giovanna Tornabene—an attractive woman who speaks nearly flawless English, who attended university in Palermo, studied in London, and then returned home to help run Gangivecchio—rushes into the dining room, welcomes us warmly (we've exchanged e-mail messages), apologizes for being distracted tonight because her mother isn't feeling well, and invites us for lunch tomorrow at the abbey. After consulting briefly with her brother, who owns the inn and presides genially over the proceedings from a table in the corner, she hurries out again.

At noon, we arrive, as instructed, at the abbey, where Giovanna greets us and apologizes again: Fortunately, Mama is feeling better today, but now twenty or thirty people have called to make reservations for lunch, she's short on help ... She's an immensely appealing person and the obvious strain under which she's operating (feeding thirty strangers a five-course lunch is not the same as throwing together a little meal for the family!) makes her all the more sympathetic.

She shows us to a table in the dining room overlooking the mountains, lights a cigarette, opens a bottle of white wine, fills our glasses, and begins to talk about the inventiveness and freedom of Sicilian cuisine ("There are no great chefs to imitate and follow, no strict rules, no recipes, it's all about making something up with whatever you have in the kitchen. Today, for example, I had no parsley for the pasta sauce, so fine, I used celery ..."). But all that freedom, in this case, does not include the liberty to finish a thought or a sentence. (In that way, running Gangivecchio seems a little like raising quadruplets who have all reached the crawling stage at once.)

Suddenly afraid that the bread might be burning, Giovanna races back to the kitchen, then reappears after a while to talk about the new cookbook she's begun, one which will be based on—and take its recipes from—the relationship between cuisine and history, family history in particular and Sicilian history in general: the festive dinner that was served at her grandparents' wedding, what people ate during World War II when food shortages challenged the most resourceful cooks. Then Giovanna remembers something else that needs to be done, which she fears no one is attending to, and jumps up from the table. Apologizing yet again—though really, we're the ones who should be apologizing for distracting her at a moment that so plainly demands her unbroken concentration—she invites us to look around the abbey.

We wander down a long, wide corridor, past an informal display of handmade farming implements and pause to gaze out the window at the courtyard beneath—at its archway, its grand and graceful proportions, at the morning sunlight striking its rosy, blistered walls, at its romantic aura of noble age and picturesque disrepair. Sections are under construction, new building projects are in progress all over the farm. Across from our window, a large section of roof is covered with metal.

Giovanna comes up us behind us.

"It's so beautiful," we say.

"Yes," she agrees, sighing. "But the roof ... several winters ago, it collapsed under the weight of the snow. And I have been trying to fix it, but because the abbey is, how do you say, protected by the government?..."

"A historical landmark?"

In Gangivecchio

"Yes, a historical landmark. Because the abbey is a historical landmark, I am not allowed to just put up roof tiles, I have to find tiles that are at least a hundred and fifty years old, that match completely the imperfections, the discolorations of the ones that are already there. It's very difficult to find such tiles, and extremely costly, so it can't be fixed."

"But certainly it's all worth it," I say. "The place is so extraordinary."

"Yes," she says. "It's worth it. But it's so expensive." She looks past us out the window at the abbey, the gardens, the land that she so clearly loves, and she sighs again, more deeply this time. It occurs to me that, notwithstanding the armies of strangers arriving to be fed and housed, life at Gangivecchio must, at times, get lonely.

"It's so beautiful here," she repeats, then smiles ruefully. "And it's so much work."

CHAPTER NINE

The Leopards

A friend in Palermo has another story about the history of the Tornabene family, one that does not involve cuisine.

"I remember, I was a girl," she says. "Maybe fifteen. And I went somewhere, to see friends, maybe, and there was a girl there, a young woman from the Tornabene family. She was very beautiful, and she had fallen in love with a boy, a very handsome boy. She wanted to marry him, maybe she had already tried to run away with him, but her family would not allow it, because the boy was not from an aristocratic family, his father was some sort of craftsman. And she was obeying her family, she was going home to her mother, giving up everything, youth, love, sex, because the family insisted. On the night I saw her, she was brushing her hair, she had very beautiful long hair, she was brushing her hair and weeping, tears were running down her cheeks. I'll never forget that image of her, brushing her long hair and weeping, brushing and weeping...."

Intensely romantic, theatrical and melancholy, this image of the Sicilian Rapunzel, of the Palermitan Juliet forbidden to marry her working-class Romeo is powerful and memorable partly because it so precisely mirrors the popular image of the Sicilian aristocracy. The enduring fascination of the Sicilian nobility extends far beyond the island itself. It draws travelers and tourists to photograph the decaying baroque palazzi in the historical centers or (as in Bagheria, a suburb of Palermo) the grand mansions that, like their inhabitants, are doggedly holding onto the vestiges of their pride amid the humbling reality of the grisly modern housing blocks surrounding them. Dreams of long-gone princes and baronesses inspire motorists to pull off the road and contemplate the rambling mansions and walled farms being remodeled or left to rot at the edge of vineyards and grazing lands.

More than any other surviving aristocracy except perhaps for the British royal family and until recently the rulers of Monaco, the faded Sicilian nobility inspires the romantic fantasies not only of those who live here or who long to visit, but also of many who have no intention of ever setting foot on the island. The substance of this dreamy fascination has been generated not by history or by contemporary reality (outside Italy, few people could name one Sicilian *principe* or contessa) but by literature, by one writer, one novel—Giuseppe Tomasi di Lampedusa's *The Leopard*—and by the somewhat shapeless but popular film that Luchino Visconti made from Lampedusa's book, starring Burt Lancaster in the title role of Don Fabrizio, the Prince of Salina, the proud leopard who watches the old order disintegrate and surrender to the imperatives of progress, social change, and populist revolution.

First published in 1958, translated into dozens of languages, the book became an international best-seller, its reputation partly fueled by the romance of its aristocratic author's idiosyncratic literary career. Lampedusa mulled over his projected novel for a quarter of a century but did not begin writing the book until he was sixty. He composed almost nothing besides *The Leopard*. Informed by an editor that his work was not good enough to be published, he died before the novel was printed and acclaimed as a masterpiece.

A brochure funded by the European Union maps the borders of the Parco Letterario Giuseppe Tomasi di Lampedusa and outlines a series of walks past the places in Palermo that Lampedusa frequented and that he described in his novel, including the route that Don Fabrizio's family takes as they travel down from their home in the hills to attend a glamorous ball in the city. Near the Piazza Ungheria is a café where the writer is supposed to have spent mornings working on his book. During the time it takes me to consume a small dish of pistachio ice cream in the back room, we see two literary pilgrims enter, poke around, and leave, obviously disappointed and bewildered by the café's gleaming chrome interior and apparently unaware that, as the brochure explains, the author's actual haunt was next door to its current namesake—and no longer exists.

Yet unlike other novels that have inspired cultish veneration and devotional travel itineraries, *The Leopard* truly *is* a work of genius. Beautifully written, at once lyrical and precise, it has enjoyed the rare good fortune of having been expertly translated into English by Archibald Colquhoun. Though relatively brief, it deftly and telescopically encompasses a long span of time—the maturity, the decline, and the death of its hero, the Prince of Salina, and the sweeping historical changes (the arrival of Garibaldi and his forces, the unification of Italy, the end of the rigidly stratified feudal system, and the rarefied, aristocratic milieu in which the prince has lived) that take place during his lifetime.

One reason why the book inspires such fervent admiration is the enormously moving and (we feel) accurate way in which it conveys how swiftly time seems to pass and the shocking surprises it delivers, the immense and humbling chasm between our hopes and expectations—and what ultimately occurs. Also the novel functions—and can be read—on a number of different levels. Most people remember the Salinas's sumptuous Sunday lunch and the gargantuan baked *maccheroni,* possibly one of the greatest descriptions of food in all of literature; I thought of it several times during our own lunch at Gangivecchio. And what also lodges in the reader's mind is the passionate love affair and the ultimately unhappy marriage between the prince's nephew Tancredi and Angelica, the beautiful daughter of the mayor of the town in which the prince's ancestral estate is located.

But what fewer readers remember is how profoundly this marriage symbolizes the decay of the old social order; and even fewer may notice the fact that the bride's father, Don Calogero, represents a type—ambitious, financially astute, devious, and manipulative—who will reappear among the small-town Mafia dons in the fiction of Leonardo Sciascia. On rereading the book, you may find that it has much more to do with politics and with its specific historical setting than you might have recalled; in fact, it can almost be studied as a textbook (of a certain sort) on the history of Sicily in the mid-nineteenth century. But finally what gives the book its particular—and particularly Sicilian—character is its ability to accept and embrace the paradoxical, to celebrate and at the same time critique a system of values that is simultaneously heroic and decadent, admirable and insupportable, suffocating and liberating.

These paradoxes, this romantic and ironic nostalgia suffuses the sites on which the old order has left its mark. In the Kalsa district of Palermo, not far from where the appropriately forlorn office of the Lampedusa Institute dispenses its brochures, is the Palazzo Mirto, the former home of the princes of Lanza Filangeri. Perhaps it has something to do with the hour (late afternoon), or the time of year, or the fact that we're the only visitors, but the palace is kept in total darkness; possibly, there's some concern that the sun might damage the fragile pastel silk upholstery of its sofas and chairs.

One ornate interior flows into another, and a guard follows us from salon to salon, from parlor to parlor. As we enter each room, he switches on the lights, illuminating the crystal sconces, the massive Murano glass chandeliers, then switches them off the moment we leave. Our eyes have to keep adjusting to the change, to the brilliance and then the blackness. After-images from the previous room float, disorientingly, in the gloom before us, all of it adding to the magical, slightly disturbing impression that the place has been slumbering, alone with its ghosts and its shadows, and is waking up, grudgingly, little by little and only briefly, to greet and then dismiss us.

Faded and more than slightly tatty, the decor could hardly be more theatrical or more revealing of the sweet, vanished dream in which its former owners passed their nights and days. The dark embossed leather that covers the walls of the smoking room seems to have absorbed—and to emit—not merely a faint whiff of the tobacco that the men enjoyed after dinner, but a dim echo of their laughter and their conversation. Furnished with scrolled and filigreed black lacquer settees and fanciful Chinoiserie, surrounded by eighteenth-century murals depicting a landscape of pagodas and temples, the charming Salottino Cinese is like a miniature stage set for an operetta set in an Asian garden. In a courtyard visible through the windows of a sitting room is a fountain encrusted with sea shells arranged in rococo patterns that—evidently, the funerary aura of the palace has begun to get to me—evoke the gaudy ossuaries that, in certain catacombs and chapels, explore the decorative potential of the cranium and the femur. And from the grand piano, photographs of the dead prince and princess stare at us with unreadable, distant expressions—as removed, as melancholy, as turned inward as the dying prince in the final pages of Lampedusa's novel.

All over the island, it's easy to find evidence of the nobility's predilection for, indeed their insistence on, surrounding themselves with beauty, a desire that often manifested as a febrile enthusiasm for collecting. In small towns and large cities are house-museums that attest to this or that baron's taste, this or that prince's eye for kitschy figurines, or ancient coins, or (more rarely) great art. The Casa Museo di Antonino Uccello in Palazzolo Acreide possesses one of the island's foremost collections of traditional and folk art—tastefully chosen and aesthetically displayed objects that include kitchen and farming equipment, cheese molds and infant cradles, dolls and stage sets for the puppet theater, votive objects, charms against the evil eye, reverse paintings on glass, and hand-tinted photographs of long-dead men and women.

Sciacca's Palazzo Scaglione contains ceramics, bronze statuettes, an eighteenth-century crucifix carved from ivory and mother-of-pearl, and a huge selection of paintings by anonymous Sicilian artists, arrayed in yet another palace furnished with divans whose stuffing is beginning to poke through the figured upholstery, yet another grand piano on which framed photos of the house's former inhabitants stare gloomily at the passing strangers who represent the diminished state to which their glory has been reduced. When I ask the guard at the Palazzo Scaglione about the museum's founder, he replies that he was some kind a rich landowner, some sort of baron—an answer which provokes a long and heated discussion with the woman washing the tile floors, about what rank of the nobility, precisely, Francesco Scaglione held.

In Cefalù's Museo Mandralisca, an institution founded by a nineteenth-century aristocrat, the Baron Enrico Piraino di Mandralisca, are a series of family portraits that could serve as illustrations for Lampedusa's novel, a collection of Greek and Roman coins, the splendid fourth-century B.C. vase depicting the tuna salesman that so resembles the fishmongers at Catania, and (as a sort of grand finale) a roomful of taxidermy that looks decidedly the worse for wear, sadly unimproved by the decades that have passed since the baron acquired these hapless stuffed creatures. There is also a group of partially restored baroque paintings; little squares of canvas have been cleaned, while other areas have been sectioned off and marked for restoration but left uncompleted. I've never seen anything like it in a museum before, and when I ask a young curator about it, she shrugs resignedly—what can you do?—and says, "The money ran out."

In considerably better shape is Antonello da Messina's "Portrait of an Unknown Man," a work that—like his more famous "Annunciation" in Palermo's Galleria Regionale di Sicilia—displays the ways in which he combined the lapidary pictorial techniques of the Flemish painters (Vasari claimed, probably erroneously, that da Messina studied with van Eyck) with the sensibility and the sensitivity of Italian Renaissance por-traiture to create works whose magnificence comes partly from the paradox they present: How could something so painstakingly, so exquisitely crafted—how could a painting that must have taken so much time—nonetheless capture an expression that seems so fleeting, so personal, so revealing and mysterious?

Something about the interface between great art and funky taxidermy, between having the money and power to acquire a portrait by da Messina and using that fortune to endow a museum that would eventually lack the funds to finish restoring its own collection, suggests a vision of the nobility much like the one we get from Lampedusa. Oddly, or perhaps not so oddly at all, it's also similar to the atmosphere that suffuses *Gli Ultimi Gattopardi (The Last Leopards),* a book of photographs of con-temporary Sicilian aristocrats by Shobha, a photojournalist based in Palermo, and the daughter of the great Sicilian anti-Mafia photographer, Letizia Battaglia.

What's most immediately striking about Shobha's subjects is their theatricality. Nearly every one of the men, women, and children she portrays is acutely aware of—and actively performing for—the camera. Many seem to be playing roles borrowed from the ennui-and-angst-ridden early films of Antonioni, and to be using their wealth, their physicality, and their sexuality as raw material for some ironic, self-mocking private drama. So few of the pictures capture people doing what you imagine they'd be doing without the photographer present that it becomes hard to imagine what they *would* be doing alone, unobserved, in a room.

In one image, a young woman points a rifle at the ceiling while a man monitors her watchfully and an older man stares at the camera, as if checking for its reaction. A woman poses in a bubble bath, wearing only a bracelet and a wristwatch, smoking a cigarette and talking on her cell phone, while the mirror beside her delivers the reverse image of her studied faux-relaxation. Three women surround a swimming pool; grandma lounges nonchalantly on the deck, her middle-aged daughter stands tensely, braced against the base of the diving board, while *her* daughter, naked but for a thong, dives into the water, her arms and legs spread, grinning at the viewer. Details of dress and gesture—a ring, a fur collar, an evening gown—seem calculated and selected entirely for effect, chosen to telegraph their wearer's simultaneously larger-than-life and anxious personality.

A warm, vibrant woman in her forties, with an electric energy so intense that even her thick blond hair seems independently animated, Shobha—who has written about the connection between the church and the Mafia and who has reported for European magazines and newspapers from as far afield as Cuba, Eastern Europe, Central America, and the United States—lives with her boyfriend, Paolo Falcone, in a light-filled, rambling apartment not far from the Piazza San Domenico. Their place is crammed with art books (Paolo is the founder and curator of the Micromuseum, an alternative exhibition space for artists), plants, computer equipment, African drums (at university, Shobha studied to be a musician), statues of the Buddha, small shrines, votive candles, bright shawls, and curios brought back from Shobha's many visits to India, where she converted to Hinduism more than twenty years ago.

"I never tell the people I photograph what to do," she tells me, "where to stand, how to act. It took a while for the people you see in the book to trust me. But after awhile they did. And as soon as I'd arrive, they'd say, 'Oh, let's do this, let's do that.' The most dramatic shots were always their idea. They were always performing, acting, but that's what they do. So much of their lives is theater." She laughs. "It's almost like their *jobs.*"

One of the more flattering photos in the book is of a handsome young couple; the man sits at a table, holding a glass of red wine, while his barefoot wife, tanned and sinewy in a perfect little black dress, walks confidently across a tile floor with a wine glass of her own. They are, Paolo and Shobha explain, Alessio and Francesca Planeta, who have turned their ancestral estate near Sciacca into a thriving vineyard that produces some of Sicily's best wine.

Later, at lunch at a restaurant not far from their apartment, Paolo orders a bottle of Planeta's La Segreta; it's not even

Planeta's best or costliest vintage, he tells us, it's their middle-level white. Even so, it's terrific—dry, complicated, delicious. And with every mouthful it becomes clearer that the history of the Sicilian aristocracy is not merely one of steady decline, of defensiveness, boredom, decadence, and conservatism. If the desire, the talent, and the inspiration are there, they can write a great novel, found a great restaurant, acquire a great painting—and even make a fabulous bottle of white wine.

CHAPTER TEN

Palermo

Walking through the streets of Palermo with Letizia Battaglia, I've temporarily stopped worrying that I'm missing something important, that I'm only seeing the surface, the deceptively obvious. And in fact the city she's showing me is more layered and complicated than what we've seen during our last few days here—that is, before we arranged to meet and walk around with Letizia, whose photographs I have long admired, and whose show I saw last fall at a gallery in Manhattan.

In the days since we've arrived, we've visited all the art sites and tourist spots, seen the mosaics at the Palatine Chapel and La Martorana, the tombs of the Norman kings at the monumental cathedral, admired the baroque exuberance of the Chiesa del Gesù, made a sort of Serpotta pilgrimage to the churches and oratories that the sculptor encrusted with plump naked cherubs and dense depictions of biblical and historical

Church facade, Palermo

FRANCINE PROSE

scenes. We've heard the hubbub of the city (Palermo is very noisy, even by Italian-city standards) muted the minute we entered the cloister of San Giovanni degli Eremiti, a garden that makes you feel as if you've been magically transported across the Mediterranean to North Africa, or westward to southern Spain.

We've been to the archaeological museum with its huge collection of artifacts from western Sicily; in fact it's my favorite sort of museum: old-fashioned, musty, nothing user-friendly or interactive, the exhibits labeled and identified by little cards lettered in spidery, faded handwriting. We've walked through the markets and up the avenues, strolled the fashionable shopping district to the north of town, and gotten lost in the twisted lanes and cul-de-sacs of the medieval quarters.

Most enjoyably, we've spent a morning in the Orto Botanico, strolling along the wide avenues lined with palms, peering into the elaborate greenhouses, circling the pond, examining the exotic species of cactus that have been lovingly tended and preserved, marveling over the gargantuan, serpentine banyan trees and the dense groves of bamboo. Goethe called the Botanic Garden "the most wonderful spot on earth," and it was there that he was inspired to begin rereading *The Odyssey* and to write the first draft of a play about Nausicaa. In the centuries since Goethe's visit, the gardens became increasingly neglected and desolate. And it's partly Letizia Battaglia's work as a community activist that helped revive the Botanic Garden after its decline, during the 1970s, into a squalid, refuse-strewn, overgrown haven for neighborhood drunks and junkies.

In fact, the city seems in every way less sinister and menacing than it did in 1992, when we first visited—though perhaps what we're feeling has something to do with our own relief at not having to spend every waking minute rescuing our kids from the lethal onrush of traffic. But it's not just us. Palermo itself seems changed. It's claimed that the narcotics trade has declined since its peak in the early '90s, though, while we're here, the local paper carries a story about a drug stash discovered inside a statue of the Madonna.

In any case, Palermo seems to be doing its best to make us feel that we have somehow managed to be in the right place at the right moment. We arrive at La Martorana just in time to see the women getting their grocery bags blessed by the priest. As we walk into the twelfth-century chapel of San Cataldo, a group of young French seminary students touring Sicily are so moved by the church's austere beauty that they burst into song, a Renaissance liturgical hymn they chant in perfect four-part harmony. As we enter the Church of Santa Maria della Pietà, in the Kalsa district, a young man has just begun to practice, on the harpsichord, a transcribed version of Bach's double violin concerto. Most of the time, these days, the Oratorio del Rosario di San Domenico is kept closed, but as we approach, a young art restorer is unlocking the door in order to show the place to a young woman he is clearly hoping to impress—and he cheerfully lets us in.

It's also possible that the difference we feel this time has something to do with the fact that we're not exactly going out of our way to seek out the city's dark side. We've decided not to return to the Catacombe dei Cappuccini, where the dead of

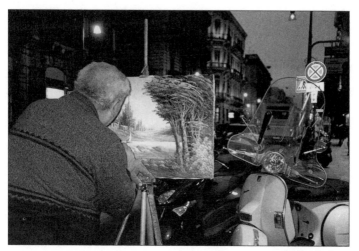

Palermo, some of whom have been in these underground passages since the end of the sixteenth century, are arranged by age and profession; many of them still sport the military uniforms, the ruffled caps, the fancy coats and dresses they wore to their graves. One especially ghoulish corpse is nicknamed the "Sleeping Beauty," a small girl so perfectly preserved by some forgotten, occult embalming technique that, it's said, she doesn't look as if she's dead, but merely sleeping. Or so they say. Frankly, it seemed to me she looked quite dead.

Last time, we went early in the morning. No one was around. As soon as we descended the first few steps that led down into the catacombs, the heavy door slammed shut behind us, plunging us into near total darkness. I was designated to find the light or get help, and as I groped my way back toward the door, I saw, in a small cell off the corridor, a dour, forbidding monk, sitting motionless and silent, his hand outstretched for the offering that persuaded him to switch on the lights. Eventually, the spookiness was ameliorated by the gang of giggly high school kids who used the catacombs as a hangout in which to flirt and grab a last minute smoke before school started.

All in all, the experience had been formidably creepy. Once was definitely enough, and besides ... maybe it's the fact that I'm older, or maybe it has something to do with the horrors of recent history, but death no longer seems like an abstraction that we can admire from a distance—to be precise, the distance between the dead and the living—as we contemplate what death has done to the citizens of Palermo, men and women and children who had once lived and breathed, just like us.

A compact, energetic, smoky-voiced woman who, in her youth, must have been even more of a beauty than she is now, Letizia Battaglia meets us in our hotel lobby, plunks herself down on a couch ... *allora.* Lighting a cigarette, she tells us that we should be talking to other people—that is, to other people besides herself, people who could give us a more positive, hopeful view of what's happening in Sicily and, for that matter, throughout the rest of Italy. Surely, there must be someone who could put a more optimistic spin on the current right-wing government, on what Letizia sees and laments as the new culture of greed, corruption, and rampant speculation that has essentially replaced the old culture of Mafia violence that she has devoted much of her life to fighting.

"I have no longer much hope," she says. "People are tired of fighting, we've lost the hope that we can win. In a way, it was easier to fight against the old violence—the murders, the assassinations—than the new violence, which is all about money and banking. The Mafia's smart, they know they don't have to kill people ... well, not much ... anymore. Now it's all about money. If a new road or a school is being built, it's not because we really need that road or that school, but because the construction is lining the pockets of the Mafia. The Mafia used to think they had to kill us, but now they know they can just *buy* us, little by little. The government is still infiltrated by the Mafia, but it's all become so civilized that it's much harder to identify and to fight. The biggest Mafioso in the government right now is an extremely cultivated man, a collector of antiquarian books...

"It's so much harder to have hope, to find that *possibility* of being free...." She sighs. "I can't find anything to photograph anymore. I used to go out and take pictures wherever I found poetry, wherever I saw that combination of something old and something new. When I took pictures of young girls, I'd see their dreams.... I was taking pictures of that dream. But now I can't find that dream. Or the dream's all about money."

It's painful to consider the possibility that Letizia Battaglia might have stopped taking photographs. Because she's an important artist—no one else has her eye, her vision; no one else is doing what she's doing. To call her Sicily's greatest photographer seems inaccurate only in that it seems too limited, too provincial. Her lyrical, unflinching, and hugely sympathetic pictures are universal in their resonance and their significance, and have been published and exhibited all over the world. Wholly original, they nonetheless bring together a number of traditions. Like the pictures of Eastern European Gypsies taken by Josef Koudelka (a friend of Letizia's and a formative influence on her work) they capture moments that suggest complex narratives and provide glimpses of the histories that their subjects share, of whole worlds of experience and of subtle nuances that fascinate and elude us; like Helen Levitt's street photographs, they catch city people—and especially the poor—in the act of expressing their tough, irrepressibly human selves; like Weegee's crime-scene shots, they portray the weirdly frozen tableaux arranged by death and violence, though Letizia's pictures—unlike Weegee's—have a gritty, grainy quality suggestive of early Italian neorealist films and of the way that time scratches and pits the walls and buildings of Palermo.

Married young, partly to satisfy her family's expectations and to escape their restrictive control, Letizia had three daughters, and in her thirties left her husband ("I took nothing from him," she says proudly) and became a journalist for a Palermo newspaper; later she moved to the mainland to work there as a photographer. On her return to Sicily, she began taking the astute and impassioned shots of her Palermo neighbors that compose her early work, and which (together with her later photos) can been seen in her book, *Passion, Justice, Freedom.*

The grisly realities of daily life in the 1960s and '70s were such that (Letizia could hardly help noticing) more and more of her street photos were turning out to be images of bloodied corpses, of men and women assassinated by the mob, and of their grieving families. Perhaps the most remarkable—the most unusual—thing about these pictures is how eloquently they convey great tenderness for the helplessness and the terrible awkwardness of the dead, profound compassion for the agony of the living, combined with a frank curiosity and an almost incandescent outrage about the waste, the cycle of violence, the pointless loss of human life—the reasons why the dead got that way. Eventually, she acquired a police radio, which enabled her to race to the crime scenes before the bodies had been removed and the dark puddles of blood sponged from the streets.

Looking at Letizia Battaglia's photography is, in certain ways, like reading the novels of Leonardo Sciascia. It's not merely that both artists have concerned themselves with the extent to which the open and covert operations of the Mafia have influenced the daily lives and the character of the Sicilian people. It's also the intelligence and care with which both Sciascia and Battaglia render the Byzantine complication and subtlety of that influence—pervasive, omnipresent in the community, unmentionable, oppressive—unsurprisingly different from the way in which Mafia violence has been portrayed by Hollywood: a bunch of wise guys (goofy or courtly, psycho or coolly business-savvy) whacking each other and going to the mattresses.

Letizia's art both fueled and was fueled by the anti-Mafia struggle in which she was involved—a campaign with its own saints, heroes, and martyrs, most notably the courageous government prosecutors, Giovanni Falcone and Paolo Borsellino, both of whom were killed by the mob. Falcone was murdered, together with his wife and three of his bodyguards, in the spring of 1992, when his car was blown up as he drove on the freeway from the Palermo airport toward the city. That same summer, Borsellino was blown up by a car bomb as he made his weekly visit to his mother; the explosion blew off the entire front of the building and shattered nearly all of its windows.

During this grim period in Palermo's history, Letizia became an increasingly vocal and visible presence. She was elected to the Palermo City Council and later the regional parliament, started a shelter for battered women and a woman's publishing collective, and sparked campaigns to clean up (figuratively and literally; her activities included organizing teams to collect garbage) some of Palermo's poorest, most despised and neglected neighborhoods. In 1979, she photographed the Italian Prime Minister Giulio Andreotti, on a visit to Palermo, greeting Nino Salvo, a well-known Mafioso—tangible proof of the mob connection that was common knowledge but which the minister denied. Letizia's photo became an important piece of evidence in Andreotti's 1993 trial on charges of corruption— charges of which he was eventually acquitted; she received death threats, her life was often at risk—and yet she kept taking pictures.

Talking to Letizia, you quickly realize how much emotion and energy she both expended on—and got back from—that struggle. So it's disturbing but not surprising to hear her say that the new mood of the country, and the Mafia's canny shift from car bombing to government lobbying, entrepreneurial speculation, and high-level influence peddling has somehow sucked the life and the blood out of the people's will to combat it—and, in the process, to better the condition of their own lives. Still, the history of that campaign, and its ongoing legacy, is so much a part of Letizia's experience that walking through the streets of Palermo with her is essentially like being taken on an anti-Mafia tour of her native city.

When we mention that we're changing hotels to stay at the Grand Hotel et des Palmes, the nineteenth-century villa-turned-hotel where Wagner stayed while finishing *Parsifal*, where a number of guests (including the French symbolist writer Raymond Roussel) committed suicide or died under sketchy circumstances, and where the Baron Castelvetrano lived in seclusion for fifty years, as penance for a murder, Letizia begins to expound on the hotel's Mafia past. Lucky Luciano used the elegant belle epoque establishment as his headquarters, and in 1957 crime bosses from Italy and the United States convened for several days in the Sala Wagner to discuss the best ways to more efficiently systematize their organization and to parcel out the international heroin trade.

"There's a guy in the bar who was there in those days," Letizia tells me. "He knows all about it, you should try and find him, though maybe he's not talking about it anymore. Maybe the hotel's trying to downplay all that." In fact, the bartender doesn't look old enough to have been born during Lucky Luciano's lifetime, and we can't quite figure out how to ask the rather stodgy desk clerk if there's anyone around who'd like to have a little chat about the hotel's notorious Mafia clients. Still, there is something about the place that makes you wonder about the table full of meticulously groomed, middle-aged men talking business over breakfast, while at the next table their bodyguards, who outnumber them two to one, closely monitor the activity—every motion anyone makes—in the mirrored, gilded salon.

As I walk through the old part of the city with Letizia, she stops every few feet, sometimes in the *middle* of the street, in heavy traffic. She's fully focused, intent and oblivious to the crowds of pedestrians or the cars streaming around her as she points out some landmark, something we might have missed … this successful business, that popular theater whose owner is friendly with Mafia leaders. An acquaintance stops and greets her. "How's the revolution going?"

"What revolution?" says Letizia.

Pasted to one lamppost is a poster advertising an upcoming lecture by a lawyer, an old man with a very long white beard. "He's a very good man," Letizia remarks. "His son was a policeman, and the son and his pregnant wife were killed. Murdered, brutally murdered. So this guy took a vow that he would not cut his hair or his beard until he found out the truth about what had happened to his son and daughter-in-law."

"Did he ever find out?"

"No," she says. "But he's old now, so his hair and beard aren't growing so fast anymore."

As we pass the Church of San Domenico, she grabs my arms and stops me. "This is where they held Falcone's funeral," she says. "And it was very sad, because of course Borsellino was there, and of course he knew—everyone knew—that he was next, that his time was coming, that they would kill him soon.…" She pauses. "People don't always want to remember," she says. "It's too hard. There was a tree in the neighborhood where Falcone and Borsellino grew up, it became a kind of shrine … people would leave things on the branches, leave offerings at the base of the tree. But it was too painful for the people in the neighborhood, and finally they just cut the tree down."

Over lunch, she asks what we've seen during our time in Palermo. When she asks if we've been to the Galleria Regionale in the Palazzo Abatellis—the Renaissance palace redesigned by the gifted Venetian architect Carlo Scarpa—we tell her how impressed we were by "The Triumph of Death," a huge, ferociously animated fifteenth-century fresco depicting Death as a skeleton riding a horse that's essentially a ribcage with legs. The ground beneath the horse's hooves is littered with the corpses of aristocrats and church officials whose gray, lifeless faces have been painted with a palette entirely different from the one used to portray the pink flesh of the living men and women who play the lute and gather beside a splashing fountain, unaware of the fate that awaits them. A few of the figures are depicted at the moment of being struck by Death's arrow, at the very instant of shock and realization; each separate death reflects (as it does in reality) the character and the personality of the individual who is dying. One side of the painting is a self-portrait of the artist, who, brush in hand, seems to be gazing at the viewer, no matter where the viewer is standing.

Letizia shudders and shakes her head. "What did you like about it?" she asks.

"It's ... amazing," I say lamely. It seems far too difficult to attempt to explain that the fresco, like her photographs, embodies what from the start I have been hoping to find here in Sicily: that Sicilian gift for extracting beauty from the harshest and most painful truths, for compelling death to admit its debt and allegiance to life, for creating an enduring—a vital and living—masterpiece that, by its very existence, contradicts the grim determinism of its title.

"I don't like it all," Letizia says, waving her hand dismissively. "I like the 'Eleanor of Aragon.'" Bunching her fingertips, she glides them down in front of her face, as if to smooth and reorganize her own lively features into the placid, bemused, sphinxlike impassivity of Francesco Laurana's fifteenth-century marble bust of a young woman. "*That,* I think, is beautiful."

"So what *should* we see in Palermo?" I ask.

"The most beautiful, the most *important* places to see are the two churches, La Magione and Santa Maria dello Spasimo." Both churches, she explains, were heavily bombed—all but completely destroyed—during World War II; both are in the Kalsa district, one of the most desolate areas of the city, a neighborhood that has only recently begun to see a revival that promises to clean up the rubble still remaining from the war, the decay and demoralization that were the by-products of the drug and Mafia violence of the last half century. Both churches, Letizia continues, have been restored. Spasimo, in particular, was rebuilt by the people of Palermo, by artists, by Letizia and her friends, by her political allies, by neighborhood residents. It is now used as a school for jazz musicians and as a cultural center, with performance and exhibition spaces available to artists.

"Those are things you can't miss," she says. "You can't leave Palermo without seeing them."

It takes me almost thirty-six hours to understand why Letizia had such a near-allergic reaction to our mention of the fifteenth-century fresco. One morning, I wake up and real-ize: At this point, she's just not in the *mood* for a work of art entitled "The Triumph of Death," a painting that almost appears to celebrate, to exult in, human helplessness and pow-erlessness in the face of the inevitable. Her response is a little like the boredom, the vague irritation, and even dread I feel at the prospect of returning for a second visit to the Catacombe dei Cappuccini. And at the instant that all this occurs to me, I decide that—although it's our last morning in the city—we can't, after all, leave Palermo without seeing, as Letizia sug-gested, La Magione and Santa Maria dello Spasimo.

Like San Giovanni degli Eremiti, La Magione is one of those churches that has the power to make the city outside grow quiet and disappear. A palm-lined path leads to the door of the sturdy, spartan twelfth-century Cistercian chapel; off to one side is a tranquil cloister garden surrounded by arched walkways. There's a purity about the place, as if the damage it suffered during the war functioned as a crucible in which the renovations and "improvements" done on the church since it was built (the addi-tion of a neoclassic facade, etc.) were burned away. Actually, that is a crude summary of La Magione's architectural history. The writer Christopher Kininmonth's view—"One is grateful that its bombing provided the opportunity to restore it to its Norman form"—may seem a little extreme, but you understand what he means. In any event, the current restoration is so thoughtful and expert that you can't imagine that La Magione was nearly destroyed, or that it ever looked any different than it does today.

Not so Santa Maria dello Spasimo. Those who rebuilt it—not restored it so much as transformed and revitalized it—had other plans, an agenda that did not include the desire to make it look whole, fix, repaired: good as new. Wisely, they realized that its suffering—the insults it sustained during the years when it was used as a theater, a hospice for plague victims, a poorhouse, and a hospital, as well as the final coup de grâce delivered by the Allied bombing—was a significant aspect of its beauty, and an even greater part of what would give the structure its meaning and significance.

As we enter the courtyard, we can hear the sounds of practice coming from the studios of the jazz school that surrounds it. But nothing can prepare us for the extreme and singular splendor of the half-ruined church, with its wooden floor, its shattered roof, its ragged holes and empty arches through which the Sicilian sun pours in, and through which we can see startling expanses of cottony clouds and blue sky.

A tree grows up through the floor and cuts diagonally across the interior. Like the great Gothic cathedrals, like the chapels of Borromini and Bernini, it has the effect of drawing your gaze—and your spirit—upward. Except that here there is no vaulted ceiling for you to admire, or to stop you. You can keep looking higher, and then higher, toward the heavens, with nothing to come between you and the bright flash of eternity. I find myself thinking of the unfinished, roofless temples at Segesta, of Giovanna Tornabene's account of how hard it had been to fix the roof at Gangivecchio, and of Sicily's ability to cut through the frivolous and inessential and make you think of the most consequential, the most primal things: for example, the necessity, the value, the meaning of a roof.

Santa Maria dello Spasimo, Palermo

Behind the church is a garden planted with neat flowerbeds and crisscrossed with pathways; a team of gardeners is at work, transplanting, mowing, pruning. Every sound they make—the clinking of their trowels, the snip of their shears—sounds like a declaration of triumph over the forces of violence and disorder.

Like the Vietnam Veterans Memorial, like Coventry Cathedral, the complex of Santa Maria dello Spasimo has accomplished the impossible; it moves us deeply without depressing us, it commemorates and honors the lives lost during the war that nearly destroyed the church and during the years of struggle against the tendrils of Mafia corruption that worked to strangle the neighborhood and to keep it from making itself anything but a rubble-strewn breeding ground for poverty and crime. What the people of Palermo have done with

Spasimo is the essence of what I am looking for here, of what the Sicilians have, by necessity, learned how to do: to transmute the horrors of history into something extraordinary—and profoundly alive.

Howie and I look at each other. Letizia was right. It's the most beautiful place in Palermo.

CHAPTER ELEVEN

Intensity

Every detail you notice, every experience you have, every person you meet, every fact you learn makes it that much harder to generalize, to summarize, to synthesize—to say anything at all. For the more you know about anything, the more unavoidably its contradictions confront you. If I say that Sicily is beautiful, I can visualize the steel reinforcement bars poking through the sidewalk at Gibellina Nuova, the bleakness of a Palermo suburb at dusk on a chilly Sunday evening, the blight of towns like Geraci Siculo, in the Madonie Mountains, where what remains of its historic center is surrounded by a virtual fortress of cheap, unsightly, high-rise housing. If I say that even the most modern aspects of Sicily still seem authentic, unspoiled, I can see the busloads of travelers trawling the jammed, once-pretty streets of Taormina in the desperate hope of finding a sale on Prada, I can hear the British matron telling her tour group that she plans to spend the afternoon on her own, engaged in some "serious shopping." And if I say that its people are welcoming and friendly, I can instantly conjure up the suspicious, hostile glare of an old woman in Racalmuto, watching us disappear and return as we drive, in frustrating and finally useless circles, around and around her town, or the chilly stares that the unemployed young men in Noto gave us as we consulted our tourist maps and snapped our photos.

But if I were asked to pick one constant, one quality that seems dependable, immutable, endlessly available, I'd say that it was intensity. For nothing in Sicily seems withheld, done halfway, restrained or suppressed. There's nothing to correspond to, say, the ironic, cerebral remove at which a Frenchman might consider an idea or a question, or the Scandinavian distrust of the sloppy, emotive response.

After awhile, I began to realize that the way I can identify other Americans in Sicily has less to do with language and dress than with a kind of hesitance, a reticence, a fear of venturing too much and embarrassing themselves, a reluctance that I could not imagine in a group of Sicilians, no matter how far they were from home, how unfamiliar and daunting the circumstances. No tight British chuckle for these people; they laugh from the solar plexus, and when they gesture with their hands, they're in motion up to the elbows. After the enjoyable and affecting morning and afternoon we spend with Letizia Battaglia, we're so drained we go back to our hotel and lie down and don't wake up until the next morning.

All this fervor, this commitment to the intense and extreme, makes it hard to write about the place without overusing the superlative. The sun is the strongest, the lemons the sourest, the scenery most sublime, the mosaics and churches and temples the most perfectly preserved. Sicilian drivers make Roman motorists look like the overcautious, nervous young people you see sometimes gripping the steering wheel beside the disaffected, chain-smoking driving instructors in the cars marked AUTOSCUOLA. If freshness is the hallmark of Sicilian cuisine, subtlety is not; the garlic is raw and biting, the sweet and the sour compete to assert themselves, one bite of the pastry is a ticket to sugar shock.

If the Sicilians pride themselves on the fact that their Carnival is the most beautiful, the most raucous, the most joyous in Italy, they will also tell you that their Easter defines the solemnity, the fervor, the depth of emotion with which the holiday is meant to be celebrated. All over the island, processions re-create Jesus' painful progress through the stations of the cross and commemorate his sufferings on the road to Calvary.

In Trapani, where the most famous of the Easter celebrations is held, groups of men from the various professional guilds—the shoemakers, the salt workers, the barbers and hairdressers, the painters and interior decorators—wind through the streets of the old city on Good Friday. On their shoulders they carry heavy platforms on which arrangements of carved and painted eighteenth-century cypress and cork figures called *Misteri* dramatize, with tremendous expressiveness and complexity, episodes from the Passion of Christ.

In the weeks before Easter, the Chiesa del Purgatorio, where the Misteri are kept, stays open long hours. The church smells of flowers—baskets of bright blooms surround each of the Misteri, whose bases are already covered in skirts of purple satin—and of varnish. A member of the fishmongers guild is stretched out, much as he would be if he were fixing a car, beneath "The Denial"; above the fishmonger repairing and retouching the base of the statue, Peter is caught forever in the act of denying Christ, while Jesus' face expresses only the sweetest and most untroubled comprehension and forgiveness.

The statues are so detailed, so realistic, so moving—and, finally, so intense—that the cumulative effect is much like that of any of the great masterpieces of Christian art; that is, they succeed in making the story of Christ's life and death new; it's as if you never heard it before, as if you were experiencing it for the very first time. Each of the groupings succeeds in reimagining the episode it represents and, even as it emphasizes Christ's divinity, confronts you with the tragedy that marks the violent end of any human life.

You feel the immensity of the distance that Jesus travels, the gravity of the suffering that changes the innocent young man taking leave of his mother and St. John in "The Separation" into the hunched, agonized victim of "The Flagellation." Even the minor players in the drama have character and personality. Their helmets decorated with bright feathery plumes, the Romans jamming the crown of thorns on Christ's head look pleased with the results of their efforts. As Christ has his moment of sorrow and doubt in the Garden of Gethsemane, his three companions slumber soundly, unaware of the significant event transpiring just above them. As you move from the scenes preceding the Crucifixion to the Deposition from the Cross, you can watch the color of Christ's flesh change from pink to gray; it's almost as if you're watching a living being at the very moment of crossing the border between life and death.

In front of each statue, a placard explains the meaning of each scene, gives a brief history of the sculpture (several were heavily damaged in the bombing of Trapani during World War II and have since been restored, one was dropped by its bearers), and identifies the guild responsible for its upkeep and for carrying it in the procession. Yet another sign explains that the bearers of the Misteri will be hooded and will move to the music of funeral marches, in a traditional pattern: Step forward, step backward, side step—presumably designed to evoke the stumbling of Jesus beneath the weight of the Cross.

"On Good Friday," the explanation continues, "when the procession passes through the narrow streets of the old center at night, all the atmosphere of gaiety and amusement vanishes, and their place is taken by a profound sense of faith and the truth, and the old city comes to life."

Easter is still weeks away, but the intensity has already begun to build. A small boy enters the church; his father takes his hand and leads him over to their friend, the fishmonger who is working on "The Denial." The man comes out from under the statue. The two friends chat, the little boy watches them, moving even closer to his father, looking up, straining to hear, because—though there's almost no one in the church, no service is in progress—the men are talking in whispers.

In Sciacca, all the hotels are undergoing restoration or closed for the winter season. The only one that's open, a short distance out of town, is a gated complex with several buildings, manicured lawns, paths, palm trees ... it looks like a cross between a Club Med and a luxury spa you might find in Palm Springs or Tucson. Actually, it is a spa, but it's not exactly luxurious. Busloads of working-class Italians, most of them old, some of them infirm, have come to take the sulfur waters that bubble up from underground springs. (Not too far away is Monte Kronio, where Daedalus is said to have found a way to turn the steamy vapors emanating from the earth into a primitive hydroelectric plant.) For some reason, we're slow to figure out why the hotel smells like rotten eggs, why we're the youngest guests by decades and the only ones not walking around in bathrobes.

No matter. Despite the smell, which mercifully diminishes as you move away from the treatment facilities on the ground floor, the place is comfortable enough, and the elderly Italians are good company—raucous, happy to be retired or on vacation, curious about how we got there and what we're doing.

One morning, I hear a group of them saying that they're planning an expedition to some place called Il Castello Incantato—The Enchanted Castle. It's a kind of folk art monument, one of those proto-environmental sculptures that reflects the urgency with which the desire to create can enter into a farmer in Georgia, an immigrant in Los Angeles, a mailman in rural France. In this case, the Enchanted Castle is the work of one Filippo Bentivegna, better known as "Filippu di li testi," Philip of the heads, after the hundreds, maybe thousands, of heads that he carved and painted, and with which he covered his small farm on the outskirts of Sciacca.

Like that of many outsider artists, Filippo's creativity was unleashed by a brush with heartbreak, humiliation, and failure. The son of a large, impecunious family, he enlisted in the navy and later emigrated to America in search of the work that he was unable to find in Sciacca. I'll let the charming brochure available at the site tell the next part of the story:

"In America he was ill at case (sic) with those racist people and he was immediately marginalized. During this period he fell in love with an American girl and in consequence of this, he was violently knocked over by his love rival. He was very shocked by this episode and his nature deeply changed."

He returned home and, with the modest savings he'd accumulated in America, bought a farm on which he began to carve stones and trees into heads, some of which resembled people he knew. He created a magical kingdom and became its ruler; on his forays into town, he expressed his wish to be known as "His Excellency." Eventually, he fell ill and was obliged to move into Sciacca, but he kept his farm, which he visited and tended until his death in 1967.

Though we drove and they walked, the old folks from the hotel have beaten us to the Enchanted Castle. They're already strolling along its brick paths and marveling at the rows of carved heads lined up along the top of low walls, hiding in the crevices of tree trunks, buried deep inside carved grottoes, grouped along the embankments, peering at you (their faces at once full of character and curiously unexpressive) from every inch of the property.

It's art done for the pure love of art, out of the pure need to create, and without any expectation of money, fame, career.

At the Enchanted Castle, Sciacca

Humorous, grotesque, weirdly thrilling, Filippu di li testi's work goes well beyond the merely intense and crosses into the territory of the obsessive. And again, it demonstrates that Sicilian determination to make something memorable and enduring out of the experience of violence and loss.

In the middle of the farm—which now, thanks to the work of the Bentivegna Foundation and perhaps also to the proceeds from selling some of the heads to various outsider-art museums, including Musée de l'Art Brut in Lausanne, seems more like a park—is the cottage in which the artist lived. Its walls are painted with a mural of a cityscape featuring tall buildings, skyscrapers, churches, and apartment houses. In the moat that surrounds this imaginary city swim fish that, following some Darwinian imperative, appear to have consumed entire bellyfuls of smaller fish.

I can't stop looking. The elderly hotel guests pop in and out of the cottage, exclaiming over the naive, whimsical, heartfelt rendering of a memory of New York, a city which the artist so clearly loved and which—like the nameless American girl—rejected and refused to embrace him. It takes me a minute to figure out why I find the image so upsetting: It's as if I'm seeing a vision of my future, of my real life, of what awaits me when I wake from this idyll, this Sicilian dream world, and reenter the chaotic, problematic, troubled city in which I actually live.

CHAPTER TWELVE

Departures

Goethe hated Messina, at least at first. He complained bitterly about the "accursed" city that had been leveled by an earthquake four years before his visit and blamed its total devastation on shoddy construction; wishing their homes to resemble the palazzi of the rich, people had concealed their old houses behind grand, new facades that collapsed—bringing the entire structures down with them—during the quake. "Messina," he wrote, "is a very disagreeable sight and reminded me of that primitive age when Sicels and Siculians quitted this unquiet soil to settle on the west coast of the island."

In the centuries that followed Goethe's Italian journey, Messina's luck got, if possible, even worse. A cholera epidemic devastated the population in 1854. Forty years later, there was another earthquake and, in 1908, yet another, which killed 84,000 people. More recently, in 1943, the city was firebombed by the Allies, reversing, in just a few hours, the city's long and tortuous efforts to rebuild itself.

Though Messina is often a traveler's first experience of Sicily—trains and regular ferries connect it to the mainland—few would claim it as their favorite spot on the island. Little remains of the old town except for a few houses that have survived in the gaps between characterless modern buildings. The mazelike streets of the medieval town have been replaced by a grid of wide avenues that seems to encourage the most reckless and suicidal aspects of Sicilian driving technique. It's been said that parts of Trapani, also bombed during the war, resemble a de Chirico painting, but in fact it's Messina that seems most truly surreal.

A few days before we're scheduled to fly from Catania to Rome, we drive up to Messina to see the Caravaggios in the Museo Regionale. We decide to arrive on a Sunday, when the city will be quiet, easier to navigate. And though that's certainly true—the traffic is relatively civilized and relaxed—we realize at once that we've made a mistake. Of all the cities that we've seen go dormant or dead on Sundays, Messina is the most desolate. Everything is shut, the streets have a spooky, slightly dangerous feel—as if it were the middle of the night instead of a sunny Sunday morning. Our hotel insists on taking a credit card imprint before they'll let us check in; it's the only place where this has happened in Sicily. Our room is comfortable, but slightly forlorn, as if it's absorbed the collective loneliness of too many traveling businessmen.

And the Caravaggios turn out to be a major disappointment. The museum is airy and well designed, but the

Caravaggios could hardly be more infelicitously displayed. The space is cramped, the lighting poor, the restoration peculiar. The composition of "The Raising of Lazarus" is much like that of "The Burial of St. Lucy"—here, too, the figures are pressed into the bottom section of painting, beneath a simultaneously soaring and oppressive expanse of darkness—but the effect that the work produces (at least in its present surroundings) is nowhere near as powerful. Puzzled, we look at it for awhile, then move on to contemplate "The Adoration of the Shepherds." And then we just stand there, as if we're waiting for something to change, for the light to come up, for the partitions to move back, for the restorers' handiwork to undo itself. Of course, none of that happens, and we leave the museum, vaguely depressed.

But why should we have expected anything else? Though he was generously paid for "The Adoration," Caravaggio had a tough time in Messina. While he worked on "The Raising of Lazarus," he insisted that he be given as a studio a room in the local hospital and a fresh corpse to serve as a model for the dead Lazarus. It was here that he assaulted his living models, local workmen, when they complained about the cadaver's smell. It was also in Messina that he slashed his first version of the painting after it was criticized by some prominent citizens, provincials who were merely overeager to have an opinion, to seem au courant and informed. And it was here—according to Francesco Susinno's 1724 *Lives of the Messinese Painters*—that, on holy days, Caravaggio would follow a teacher named Don Carlo Pepe to watch Don Carlo's male students at play in the city arsenal, observing them with such transfixed attention that the teacher became suspicious enough to inquire what, precisely, the painter thought he was doing. Insulted, Caravaggio struck Don Carlo on the head and wounded him—and was consequently obliged to leave Messina. "In short," concludes Susinno, "wherever he went he would leave the mark of his madness."

After our trip to the museum, we have lunch in the only open restaurant we can find. I spend the rest of the afternoon in our hotel room, rereading guidebooks to see if there's anything we might be missing, something in Messina that might be open, or worth doing, on a chilly, drizzly Sunday. There isn't. And the banks of fog that keep rolling in discourage us from driving up to catch the scenic view of the city from the Via Panoramica.

On Monday morning, we're glad to leave, to head back down the coast to warm, sunny Acireale, where we'll stay until our flight to Rome. But soon it turns out that perhaps we should have taken a lesson from Goethe, whose opinion of Messina was reversed when he met the city's governor and the German consul, with whom he had such an agreeable time that he wished he had ignored his unfavorable first impression of Messina and decided to stay longer.

One afternoon—in fact the afternoon before we're scheduled to leave Sicily—I'm watching CNN in our hotel room in Acireale. They're featuring a disturbing report from the Afghan war, a press conference in which government officials announce the deaths of several American servicemen, as well as Afghan soldiers and civilians, and describe the powerful new weapons being used to blow up the enemy fighters still hiding in caves. Meanwhile, beneath the image of the military commander and the press secretary, the "crawl" bannering across the screen announces that, in the Sicilian city of Messina, a bronze statue of Padre Pio is reported to have begun weeping tears of blood.

Messina! We were just there! We left too early, just as Goethe left too early, just as we're leaving Sicily entirely too early! Why are we going to Rome when we should be driving back up north to witness a miracle?

All over Sicily—by the cash registers in tobacco stores, under the blaring televisions in family *trattorie,* on the dashboards of taxis and buses—we've seen images of Padre Pio, the simple farmer's son from southern Italy who became a Capuchin monk and, in 1918, first exhibited the stigmata, the five wounds of Jesus, on his frail body. After performing many miracles and healings and becoming the center of a large, devoted following, Padre Pio died in 1968. Fifteen years after his death, the beatification process began; in 1999, he was declared Blessed by Pope John Paul II.

And now, in the late winter of 2002, his statue has begun to weep. The tears have been sent to police laboratories for analysis, but the masses of people arriving daily at the site of the miracle aren't waiting for the results, nor is the girl who reported touching the foot of the statue and feeling a great heat, nor is the wheelchair-bound woman in Sant' Agata di Militello, who, it is said, has been cured of multiple sclerosis.

In fact, we can't stay any longer, we can't return to Messina. We have obligations, commitments, we have to get on to Rome. And yet the reports from Messina make me feel suddenly, unreasonably happy—not merely consoled, but optimistic. Perhaps what cheers me so much is the fact that, at lunch this afternoon in the port of Aci Trezza, I listened to a group of sleek Catanians discuss some computer-related business opportunity in language so technical I could hardly understand a word. And then, after my *fritto misto,* my *tiramisù,* and coffee, I have come back to my hotel room to read the news from Messina: A statue of Padre Pio is weeping even as the technocrats are buying and selling their state-of-the-art electronics.

It all seems exquisitely Sicilian: the seamlessness and grace with which the present layers itself over past, with which the ancient coincides with the modern, with which the stigmatist coexists with the scientist. The news about Padre Pio does not erase or obliterate or lie about the dispatches from the war in Asia. But it does makes you wonder what, exactly, is causing the saint to weep—to shed tears in a country, on an island that has seen countless cycles of violence and peace, of poverty and prosperity, of horror and beauty.

Perhaps I should end where I began, with Odysseus's accidental, adventurous, and ultimately pleasurable sojourn in Sicily. After Nausicaa saved the half-drowned sailor and brought him to her father's court, after Odysseus enthralled the Phaeacians with the stories of his exploits—his escape from the Cyclops and from Circe's island, his journey to the underworld, his voyage past the Sirens and though the Straits of Scylla and Charybdis—King Alcinous announced that he was sending his honored guest off with a boatload of treasure: beaten gold and bronze, food and wine, clothing, rugs and sheets to sleep on. And so, after all his perils, after the twenty years of wandering, Odysseus—with his memories of the Island of the Sun, with his hard-won wisdom, his hard and glorious experience, his precious and priceless gifts—at long last set sail for home.

CHAPTER THIRTEEN

Gifts

What, then, have I brought home with me? The gifts range from modest to large. A kitschy scrolled painting on velvet that features the word 'Sicilia' in glittery letters surrounded by representations of the cathedrals of Palermo and Monreale, a peasant cart, a palm tree, the ruins at Agrigento. A tinted vintage postcard of the smoldering cone of Mount Etna. Recipes, some new ideas about food; the inspiration and the will to keep searching for a fish store in which they will slice the swordfish thin enough for *pesce spada alla palermitana*.

And then there are the intangibles. Not long after my return, I was talking on the phone with a friend about the world situation, which, of course, had gotten no less perilous and alarming in the time since I'd left for Italy. We were discussing the folly and absolute necessity of conducting business as usual in the face of uncertainty and fear. On the surface, we focused on my friend's pressing need to call the exterminator (water bugs!) even though she was nearly paralyzed with worry about the conflict in the Middle East, and between India and Pakistan. Beneath the surface, we were really discussing the folly and absolute necessity of continuing to write (my friend is also a writer) and of trying to make art despite our concerns about the continuing survival of the planet and of civilization.

And then, as it happened, I found myself thinking of the "Ephebus of Mozia," the statue of the young man that I saw in the Whitaker Museum, on the nearly deserted island off the coast between Trapani and Marsala. I pictured it with utter clarity—its grace, its beauty, the way it seems lighted from within—and it struck me that whoever had carved it in the fifth century B.C. had done so either during a period of strife or unrest, or in a brief spell of peace between two outbreaks of violence. And yet the statue had been made, and war had indeed broken out, and the sculpture had been buried, and saved, and unearthed, and recognized as the masterpiece that it is. As I imagined it, radiant and tranquil, in its room in the museum, the very fact of its existence seemed like evidence, like a sign of what Sicily has to tell us if we are willing to listen: that it is necessary to operate on faith and to believe that what we do will, like the beautiful "Young Man of Mozia," survive and endure.

ABOUT THE AUTHOR

Francine Prose is the author of ten novels, including *Bigfoot Dreams, Primitive People,* and *Blue Angel,* a National Book Award finalist in 2000, and the recent nonfiction work *The Lives of the Muses.* Her short fiction, which has appeared in such journals as *The New Yorker, The Atlantic,* and *The Paris Review,* has been gathered in two collections, *Women and Children First* and *The Peaceable Kingdom.* Prose is also a prolific essayist; her pieces have appeared in *The New York Times Magazine, Harper's* (where she is a contributing editor), *Elle, GQ, The Wall Street Journal,* and *The New Yorker.* She is the recipient of numerous awards and honors, including Guggenheim and Fulbright fellowships, and a PEN translation prize. She lives in New York City.

This book is set in Garamond 3, designed by
Morris Fuller Benton and Thomas Maitland
Cleland in the 1930s, and Monotype Grotesque,
both released digitally by Adobe.

Printed by R. R. Donnelley and Sons on
Gladfelter 60-pound Thor Offset smooth
white antique paper.

Dust jacket printed by Miken Companies.
Color separation by Quad Graphics.

Three-piece case of Ecological Fiber putty side
panels with Sierra black book cloth as the spine
fabric. Stamped in Lustrofoil metallic silver.

NATIONAL GEOGRAPHIC DIRECTIONS

Featuring works by some of the world's most prominent and highly regarded literary figures, National Geographic Directions captures the spirit of travel and of place for which National Geographic is renowned, bringing fresh perspective and renewed excitement to the art of travel writing.